INTRODUCTION

How often have you just finished a time-consuming, fiddly task only to be told by your supposed best friend that she knows a really neat, easy way to do it? And why didn't you ask her first? How many times has your spirit been almost broken by an itsy-bitsy but remarkably colourful stain on the carpet; by a cat who finds your garden the most appealing in the entire suburb; or by a neighbour who compares the lightness of your sponge cake to a volume of the *Encyclopaedia Britannica*?

'Real people' like you and I know that we couldn't even count the times. We just accept that another 'itsy-bitsy stain on the carpet' is a certainty. *The Ultimate Book of Household Hints* removes that sense of inevitable doom. There you will find everything you ever wanted to know about the removal of carpet stains, offending cats and feather-weight sponge cakes. The information is listed alphabetically so that it is easy to find — not like the parts of a springform cake tin. The book is a panacea for domestic disasters, containing hundreds of hints and tips to make almost every aspect of home care easier.

You will know that this book is for 'real people' when we tell you that all the hints and tips have come from other 'real people' — people who have shared their triumphs with Molly Dye in her *Sunday Telegraph* column.

— The Editor

■ Borax and sugar is an effective ant poison. Mix 2 cups sugar, 1 cup hot water, 2 tablespoons borax, 2 tablespoons boracic acid. Boil for 3 minutes, cool and bottle. Place in low-sided dishes near ant trails. Replenish dishes until ants are eliminated.
■ Crushed cloves sprinkled near nest will repel ants.
■ Sprinkle talcum powder across ant trail outside nest.

ALUMINIUM
Stains and marks

■ If food burns on the bottom of pan, cover it with vinegar and add 1 tablespoon of salt. Leave overnight, empty pan and scour.
■ To prevent discolouration when cooking steamed puddings or boiling eggs, add a little vinegar, a slice of lemon or lemon juice to the water.
■ See also *Cast Iron Cookware, Saucepans.*

Polishing

Aluminium takes on a sheen if rubbed with a cloth soaked in cloudy ammonia. Polish with a soft cloth.

ANTS
Controlling the Blighters

■ Sprinkle sugar where ants will find it. Follow ant trail back to the nest. Pour kerosene, turpentine or paraffin into nest. The ants will not return, and paintwork will not be affected.

APPLES
Baking Apples

Make foil into a cup shape. Bake apples in the cups. When cooked, apples slip easily onto plates.

Instant apple sauce

Strained apple baby food makes a delicious condiment for roast pork.

APRICOTS
How to Dry Apricots

Dissolve 200 g sodium meta-bisuphite (sold at health shops) and 1.5 kg sugar in 10 litres water. Wash and halve apricots and soak them in the solution for 12–15 hours. Rinse and place on a board, cupside up, to dry in the sun. Protect from ants by mounting the board over water. Cover with gauze to protect from insects, and bring in at night or if it rains.

ARTHRITIS
Relieve That Pain

Bruise 16 small hot chillies, making sure the seeds are not exposed. Soak chillies in 225 ml brandy for 24–36 hours. Remove chillies and bottle liquid. Use 5 drops in tea or coffee twice daily until relief is obtained.

Controlling Arthritis

For six months of the year when arthritis is worst, try this remedy: Wash 3 ripe grapefruit (thick, skinned), 3 oranges, 3 lemons. Remove pips. Put the fruit and skin through a vitamiser or fine mincer. Add 200 ml water, stand overnight. Next day, pour 1.5 litres boiling water over a mixture of 50 g cream of tartar, 50 g epsom salts. Allow to cool (don't let it become cold or salts will crystalise). Mix with citrus solution and refrigerate.

    Take 2 dessertspoons on an empty stomach when you get up. Follow with a glass of warm water 10–15 minutes later.

BACON

■ Bacon wrapped in foil will not dry out so quickly in the refrigerator.
■ Coat bacon with flour before cooking to prevent shrinkage. Before cooking, prevent curling by dipping bacon in milk, or cutting the rind in several places.

BALLPOINT PENS
To Make Ink Flow

■ Remove cap, place tip in warm water for 30 minutes. Scribble while still warm.
■ Wrap pen in foil and place in a warm oven, having switched oven off. Remove when oven has cooled.
■ Place pen in direct sunlight on a piece of paper. Leave for 30 minutes and pen should work again.

BANANAS
To Prevent Browning

Peel bananas and hold under cold tap, or sprinkle peeled bananas with lemon juice or sherry, before adding to fruit salad.

Drying

Cut firm, ripe bananas lengthwise. Dry in a slow oven, turning occasionally. Cool and store in airtight containers. Alternatively, bananas can be sun-dried in very hot weather, which takes several days. Bring inside at night to protect from moisture.

Banana for the Garden

Cut these up and dig in and around gardenias and hoya. The skins will promote bright, glossy leaves.

BARBEQUE
Cleaning cooking plates

■ While the plate is still very hot, sprinkle a handful of salt on it and leave until it cools. It is then reasonably easy to clean.
■ Soak plates or grill overnight, or as long as possible, in a strong solution of Castle dishwashing powder. Just wipe clean.

For Glowing Coals

Sprinkle 1½ teaspoons of salt on your barbeque fire for glowing coals.

BATHS
Removing Stubborn Marks

Stubborn stains on baths can be whisked away by scrubbing with a slice of lemon dipped in salt, a cloth dipped in vinegar or a cloth dipped in turpentine.

Polishing

After cleaning, a sprinkle of bicarbonate of soda and a rub with a kerosene-dipped rag makes a bath shine.

Bath Salts and Essences

■ A few drops of ammonia added to the bath water makes the water feel wonderful.
■ Bath salts can be made by mixing 1 kg washing soda crystals with 70 g borax. Add a few drops of your favourite plant oil, such as oil of verbena. Keep in sealed glass jars and use 1 tablespoon in your bath.
■ Bath essence can be made by mixing 2 cups of sage leaves with lavender heads, rosemary leaves or full-blown roses and adding water. Add a pinch of salt and bring to the boil. Strain and use liquid to scent your bath water.

BATTER
Cooking Hint

Mix batter with custard powder when making fishcakes or rissoles. This binds the batter and is a good substitute for eggs.
■ See recipes under *Cooking*.

BATTERIES
New Life

Transistor radio or torch batteries can be given a new lease of life when run down by putting them in a warm oven for about an hour.

BEANS
Freezing beans without blanching

Slice and prepare beans ready for cooking, put in a sealed plastic bag or plastic ice cream container and place in freezer until needed. Do not wash them until you are ready to use them. You can take the quantity you need for a meal and put remainder back in freezer. This method can also be used for peas.

Preparing Beans

String with a potato peeler, then cut quickly with kitchen scissors.

BEDSPREADS
Fluff on chenille

Put bedspread over bed and lightly clean with the nozzle of your vacuum cleaner. This removes most excess fluff. For finer fluff, use Ezy Fabric Comb. These methods are effective on cardigans, blankets and chenille bedspreads.

BEES
Repelling Bees

■ To keep bees away from a swimming pool or barbeque pit, grow hawthorn which repels bees. The plant is only pollinated by flies, has coloured spring flowers, bright berries and grows to 3 or 4 metres in most soils and situations.
■ The flowers from the feverfew plant, which can be grown in pots, repel bees. Other repellants are tansy, thyme, garlic, laurel, wild marjoram, winter savory, wormwood and the leaves of eucalyptus.

BEESWAX
Beeswax from Honeycomb

■ For only one hive, simply cut the comb into manageable lumps, take off the cappings with a hot knife and let the honey drain out into a large clean bowl in a warm place. Keep the screens closed on doors and windows; the smell of honey attracts bees. When drained, the comb can be broken up and very gently heated until thoroughly melted, preferably over a pan of water so it does not burn. Strain through a couple of thicknesses of clean cotton or cheesecloth and allow to solidify. Any remaining honey will stick to the bottom.
■ For more than 1 hive, it's worthwhile hiring or buying a centrifugal extractor. Hiring is quite cheap. Look under Apiarists' Supplies in telephone directory.
■ Put beeswax into a clean muslin or similarly porous bag, hang up and place container underneath. Honey will run out of the wax and be strained into container.

BEETROOT
Preserving Beetroot

■ Boil beetroot until tender, peel and slice, place in airtight container and sprinkle lightly with sugar. Boil sufficient brown vinegar to cover beetroot. Pour vinegar over beetroot and make airtight. Will keep for several weeks.

■ Wash 6 beetroot. Put into boiling water to which a little salt has been added. Boil 1½ hours. Cut beetroot into slices and pack into jars.

■ Boil 600 ml vinegar, 15 g each ginger and peppercorns, 12 cloves. When boiled, add a second 600 ml cold vinegar. Pour over beetroot and cover tightly.

Keeping Beetroot Longer

Pour hot vinegar instead of cold vinegar over beetroot after slicing.

BIRDS
Stopping birds pecking at screens

Birds do this because they can see their reflections in the glass. To preserve wire screens, suspend a small piece of bright snake skin or something similar in the centre of the outside screen. Suspend by strong black thread fixed to the top and bottom of screen.

When Pigeons Nest in Pot Plants

■ To prevent pigeons nesting in verandah pot plants, fill one or two small containers with ammonia and bury in the pot.

■ Nylon fishing lines tied over the top of pots and plants will keep birds away. As their feet get tangled in the lines they will not come back again.

A Balanced Diet for Lorikeets

■ These birds enjoy a wide variety of ripe fruits such as grapes, rockmelons, pawpaws, oranges, pears and apples. Another preparation they enjoy is a nectar mix made from 1 part honey, 3 parts Heinz high protein baby cereal and 10 parts water, plus 1 teaspoon Pet Vite (available from pet food stores) per cup of nectar mix. Lorikeets prefer the artificially sweet nectar mix to other foods, which can cause dietary imbalance. For this reason it is important to feed the nectar mix sparingly, at a rate of 1 teaspoon per bird. The other foods may be given freely.

N.B. The nectar mix should not be left out for longer than 6 hours, especially in summer, as it will sour and may cause illness. (The above information comes from Sydney's Taronga Park Zoo.)

■ Lorikeets at Currumbin Bird Sanctuary, Queensland are fed on a mixture of honey, dissolved in warm water, with bread soaked in it.

Keeping Birds Away

■ Weave nylon fishing lines near the roof where the birds fly. They will take fright when their wings touch the lines.

■ Use Rentokil Bird Repellant. Place where the birds rest.

■ Silver milk bottle tops strung on thread are very effective.

Seed Bells for Budgies

Mix together small quantities of maize meal, hemp seed and canary seed in a bowl. Melt a small quantity of dripping until boiling hot. Pour in with seeds and mix together. When warm, wrap in a clean cloth, like a teatowel and mould to shape desired. Insert cup hook at top to hang the bell. When cold and hard can be given to bird. Alternatives for mixture: millet seeds, currants, chopped nuts.

BISCUITS
Biscuit-making Hints

■ If the mixture is difficult to roll because it is too soft, draw it together with floured hands, wrap in waxed or greaseproof paper and put in a polythene bag. Refrigerate 1–2 hours. The mixture will harden up and should roll easily.

■ A biscuit breaks and crumbles because (a) there is not enough liquid to bind it; (b) too much fat has been added; or (c) mixture is not kneaded lightly until smooth. To remedy, break off small pieces and roll into balls between palms of hands, remembering to flour hands. Place on a greased tray. Lightly press flat with base of tumbler and bake.

Keeping Biscuits Fresh

Put a layer of blotting paper in the bottom of the biscuit tin.

■ See recipes under *Cooking*.

BLANKETS
Storing Blankets

Place in plastic bag with cake of soap and they will be fresh and sweet-smelling when unpacked.

Hints for Washing Blankets

■ Add a teaspoon of turpentine to the final rinse. They will dry fluffy and beautifully soft.

■ Allow 3 teaspoons gelatine to one blanket. Dissolve in 300 ml hot water. Add dissolved gelatine to a tub containing enough warm, not hot, water to cover blanket. Mix well. Place blanket in tub, soak for 30 minutes, stirring occasionally. Rinse 3 or 4 times in warm water. Squeeze, shake out and hang in breeze to dry. Blanket will be clean, soft, and fluffy.

BLINDS
Cleaning Bonded Blinds

Take down blind. Do not remove from roller as the top part of a blind is usually not exposed to dirt. Immerse lower part in hand-warm water; keep flat, do not squeeze or wring. The bath is an ideal spot to do this. Scrub gently with soft brush and ordinary household soap with a little softener added to the water. Rinse with several changes of water, peg out over 2 lines, choosing a good drying day. Turn over now and then. Press with warm iron if needed.

Mildew on Bonded Blinds

The best way to remove mildew from blinds is with Sard wonder soap. Follow the instructions inside the wrapper. A liquid form is also available.

New lease of life for blinds

Paint both sides of blinds with pastel coloured plastic paint.

Keeping Venetian Blinds Clean

Use a little white furniture wax, taking care not to use too much. Rub up well before it gets too dry. This will make dusting and cleaning venetian blinds easier.

Cleaning White Blinds

Mix a small quantity of equal parts bleach and water in a bowl. Dab the braid on the blinds with a sponge dipped in this solution, thoroughly wet the blind and leave a few minutes. Prepare about 15 centimetres tepid water in a bath, add a ¼ cup of strong wash-up detergent and ⅛ cup ammonia. Place rolled blind on floor alongside the bath. Bring bottom up and over into water, sponging as you go until all the blind has been dunked except the spring end which is held in hand. Swish backwards and forwards a few times, remove and drain over line a few minutes. Do not allow to dry. Cover table with large towel and place the blind on it. With second towel, begin wiping dry at roller end, rolling up as you go. This will bring them up like new.

Mildew on Bamboo Blinds

Willow, cane and bamboo furniture is best washed with lukewarm salted water to which a little soda has been added. Use ¼ cup of salt and 1 tablespoon of soda per litre of water. Rinse well, dry thoroughly and rub lightly with linseed oil. Furniture can be protected by coating with white shellac.

BLISTERS
Prevent Blisters

To prevent blisters from forming on feet when you do a lot of walking, rub feet with methylated spirits daily for a week beforehand.

BOOKS
Mould on leather books

■ Prevent mould forming on leather-bound books by rubbing sparingly with oil of lavender.
■ Lightly dampen a cloth with eau-de-cologne and rub gently over book cover. Wipe over straight away with a clean cloth.
■ To prevent mildew forming on book covers, sprinkle a few drops of oil of cloves or eucalyptus oil on bookcase shelves.
■ Rub books with a soft cloth dipped in vinegar or lemon essence.

Yellow Smelly Books

This can happen while books are stored on shelves. Dampness is the cause. Make sure house is well ventilated. Take books out of shelf and shake pages gently. Fan pages to loosen if dampness has made them stick together. Never pack or compress books tightly together on shelves or bookcase, always leave room for air to circulate. A couple of lumps of charcoal, Silica Gel or Calcium Chloride in the bookcase, may be used to absorb moisture from air around the books. Get rid of dampness in room by heating house for a short time, then open windows and doors to let out moisture-laden air.

Silverfish in Books

Sprinkle with Epsom Salts or place a couple of camphor blocks among books. Also helps with musty smell.

Spotty Books and Pictures

Rub gently with a piece of art gum or stale white bread. Soft bread is also good for cleaning old photographs.

BOTTLES
Cleaning Inside Bottles and Vases

Fill with small balls of steel wool and soap suds. A few brisk shakes and they are sparkling.

Removing Bottle Odours

Fill with hot water and 1 teaspoon bicarbonate soda. Leave for two hours.

BRAINS
Removing Skins from Brains

Soak brains in water which contains one dessertspoonful vinegar. Leave for 10 minutes. The skin can then be peeled off easily and cleanly.

BRASS AND COPPER
Polishing and Cleaning Brass

■ Scrub with strong ammonia, then wash. Polish with a soft cloth.
■ Clean brass and copper with a mixture of salt and lemon juice, then polish with commercial cleaner.
■ Make up a mixture of lemon juice and powdered whiting or powdered Bon Ami to clean brass. Let dry and polish off. Use small brush for any patterned area.
■ Use a metal conditioner like Deoxidine to produce an 'original' finish to brass. Deoxidine being an acid, use rubber gloves and apply with Scotchbrite cloth, rinse off with water and dry thoroughly.
■ Clean and thoroughly polish brassware. Apply one or two coats of clear lacquer with soft brush. This forms a seal over brassware, keeping out air and moisture. The brass should stay clean and shining until the lacquer coating begins to wear off or crack. If carefully handled, the coat should last about a year.
■ Apply a very thin smear of petroleum jelly after cleaning brassware. It will stay clean and shining for a longer time.
■ Clean brass with steel wool impregnated with Brasso. Then spray with Mr Sheen and buff to a high gloss with a soft rag. Will not require frequent cleaning after this.
■ Use ordinary toothpaste; the cheap brands are best as they are coarser. Rub brass with stiff brush. Engraving, filigree will be cleaned. Leave paste on for a while, especially if stains are heavy, then rinse off with warm water. Polish brass with a soft cloth.

Restoring a Brass Bedhead

Wash with household ammonia and soapy water, clean with a vinegar and salt solution using 1 heaped tablespoon salt and two tablespoons vinegar to 600 ml water. Polish with pure lemon oil not lemon oil polish.

Inlaid Brass Ornaments

Soak brass in a citric acid solution. Use a 25 g packet of citric acid dissolved in 3½ litres of hot, not boiling, water in a non-metal container. Use more solution if the article is large. Soak for 5 minutes, then gently scrub with a soft old toothbrush. Rinse under a running hot water tap, pat dry and polish in the usual way. Ideal for deeply etched or inlaid brass ornaments.

For Shining Copper

To clean copper mix 2 tablespoons vinegar with 1 tablespoon cooking salt. Rub on and wash article in hot water. Dry thoroughly. Equal parts plain flour, vinegar and salt, also do the trick.

A Gleaming Copper Kettle

Rub kettle with 1 tablespoon cooking salt and 2 tablespoons brown vinegar using a flannel cloth. Wash the kettle in clean hot water and dry well. If kettle is only for display on a shelf, polish with Brasso cleaner, give a coat of lacquer and it will last for years.

BREAD
New Uses for Old Bread

■ For stuffing, croûtons and bread puddings, cut stale bread into cubes and freeze.

■ Instead of pastry, use stale bread on fruit pies by cutting bread in slices and soaking in milk or water until soft but not soggy. Prepare fruit to be used for pie. When ready, place in pie dish. Arrange bread slices on the fruit to form a covering, sprinkle with nutmeg and bake. Serve with sweet sauce or custard.

Freshening Stale Bread

■ Freshen stale bread, scones, teacakes, raisin bread, by putting on a cake cooler in frypan. Add half a cup of water, place on lid. Bring to boil and allow water to evaporate completely.
■ Wrap stale bread in a damp, clean cloth. Place in slow oven for 15 to 20 minutes. Remove and allow to cool and bread is moist again.
■ Sprinkle bread with a few drops of water, wrap in foil and heat in moderate oven for 15 minutes.
■ Heat bread rolls by putting them in a dampened paper bag and place them in a hot oven for several minutes until crisp.

To Keep Bread Moist

Always keep a slice of fresh apple or potato in the bread box. This stops bread drying out.

Breadmaking Hints

■ Do not use self-raising flour for bread or other yeast mixtures. Strong plain flour gives better results.
■ Dried yeast is just as good as fresh yeast; just use half the amount. For example, if a recipe requires 30 g fresh yeast, use 15 g dried yeast.
■ Never use more salt or sugar than recipe states. Too much can kill some or all the yeast and stops it acting properly.
■ Never add salt directly to yeast. Always sift it with the flour and allow about 25–30 g to each 500 g flour.
■ Do not treat dried yeast as you would

fresh. Instead dissolve 1 teaspoon sugar, honey or syrup in one carefully measured cupful of warm liquid. Sprinkle dried yeast on top and stir round. Leave in warm place for 10–15 minutes or until frothy. Add to flour with rest of warm liquid.

■ Never add liquid gradually. You get a more manageable dough if you add it all at once.

■ See recipes under *Cooking*.

BREADCRUMBS
Homemade Breadcrumbs

Place crusts and small pieces of bread in a very cool oven and allow them to become quite dry and straw-coloured. Place them on a board and crush with a rolling pin or put through the mincer. If stored in a screw-top jar, these crumbs will keep for several months, as all the moisture has been evaporated.

BRIDAL
Storing Bridal Dress and Veil

Wrap in blue tissue paper, then in a dry cleaner's plastic bag. Make sure the bridal finery is covered completely by the paper to exclude light. Acid-free jeweller's tissue paper can also be used.

Cleaning Bridal Veil

To clean without losing stiffness, place the veil in a pillowslip with a couple of handfuls of oatmeal and a handful of powdered magnesia. Tie top of pillowslip and shake well, so powder is spread through the veil. Leave for 24–48 hours, giving pillowslip a shake every couple of waking hours. Outdoors, gently remove veil and shake out. Do not use water or cleaning fluid as tulle will break up.

BRONCHITIS
Bronchitis Syrup

Place 6 whole eggs in basin. Pour over juice of 6 lemons. Let stand 3 days, stirring once a day. By then shells will be soft. Beat well together, crunching egg shells finely, and put through a coarse strainer. Add 300 ml rum, 250 g honey, 2 tablespoons of sugar, mix and bottle. Cork after 1 hour. Take a tablespoon 3 times a day (or a wineglassful before going to bed).

BROOMS

Sprinkle a few drops of kerosene on a soft broom. Dust and fluff is collected more easily. Apply the kerosene about once a week.

BUBBLE MIX
Recipe for Bubbles

■ One part each liquid detergent and glycerine, 5 parts water, pinch sugar. This mixture is tough and bubbles do not burst easily.
■ Two parts warm water to 1 part wash-up liquid also makes a fine bubble mix.

BURNS

Treat minor burns by rubbing the area with ice.

BUTTER
Butter Substitute

Using a rotary beater, mix 250 g margarine with a small tin of reduced cream and 1 tablespoon hot milk, added a few drops at a time. Beat until very smooth. Quantity is doubled.

Creaming Butter and Sugar

Before beating sugar and butter together, especially in winter time, stand beaters of your mixer in hot water. Quickens the process and butter does not stick to them.

CABBAGE
Avoiding that smell

■ Add a crust of bread to cabbage, or other strong-smelling vegetables while cooking.
■ Add a thick slice of lemon to cabbage or onions to prevent cooking smells.

CAKES
Mixes and Additives

■ A few teaspoons of **marmalade** added to a rock cake mixture keeps the cakes moist and gives a good colour.
■ **Sour milk** makes a lighter cake than fresh milk. Sour with a dash of vinegar.
■ Before adding **coconut** to a cake, soak it in the milk needed in the cake. Otherwise it will have a drying effect.
■ Cold **coffee** added to ginger cakes or puddings instead of milk improves the flavour and colour.
■ Gingerbread has a richer flavour and colour if you add 1 teaspoon of melted **dark chocolate** to the treacle.
■ Always **sift packet cake mix** before using, to ensure a lighter and higher cake.

High Flying Raisins

Raisins often sink to the bottom of the cake. Prevent this by rolling them in melted butter before adding to the cake.

Hints for Cooking Cakes

■ If cakes brown too quickly, put a sheet of brown paper on the oven shelf above them.

■ Cakes sink in the centre because of too much raising agent, an over-wet mixture, a too-cold oven, or because the oven door was opened and slammed shut.

■ Holes can appear in plain cakes for many reasons:
1. Fat not rubbed in finely enough.
2. Mixture stirred too much after addition of liquid.
3. Cake tin not tapped after mixture added to remove air bubbles.
4. Heavy-handed folding.
5. Uneven mixing.
6. Too much rising agent.
7. Oven temperature too high.
8. Placing mixture into tin in small quantities, which traps air bubbles.

■ If a cake burns, scrape off the burnt part and then brush with beaten egg white and dust with castor sugar. Put back in slow oven for a few minutes.

■ When making a cake covered with nuts, first dip the nuts in milk so they will not turn black.

■ Lining cake tins with aluminium foil, extending one inch above rim, makes removal of the cake much easier.

■ If a cake splits when cooking, place a damp cloth over the top as soon as it is removed from oven. Leave for a few seconds and cake will come together.

■ For a level shiny fruit cake, brush with milk before baking. Use a small pastry brush.

■ Revive a stale fruit cake by putting a thick slice of fresh bread with cake in an airtight container. Leave for two days and cake will be moist again.

Fillings for Cakes

■ **Jam**, when used as a filling, often soaks in. Lightly butter the cake before spreading jam to prevent soaking.

■ **Banana** filling: Mash a banana, add 1 tablespoon apricot jam and 1 tablespoon coconut. Beat well with a fork.

■ **Lemon** filling: Rind and juice of 1 lemon, 4 tablespoons sugar, 3 teaspoons cornflour blended with 3 tablespoons water, 30 g butter. Simmer gently for 3 minutes. Cool before using.

Icing

■ **Easy crunchy topping**: Beat one egg white until frothy but not stiff. Add half cup sugar, pinch salt and few drops vanilla. Spread over cake before baking.

■ **Crumbly Topping**: Sift 56 g flour, half teaspoon cinnamon, add 42 g brown sugar and rub in a dessertspoon of butter. Press together until crumbly and sprinkle over cake before baking.

■ Save time by sprinkling **coarse sugar** on cake before baking. Gives a rich crust.

■ Add a decorative touch by shredding milk **chocolate** over icing while still moist.

■ Sift a little **flour** over cake before icing to prevent icing running off.

■ Instead of icing a plain cake, grate a sweet **apple** over mixture in tin before baking and sprinkle over a little cinnamon and sugar. Top with chopped walnuts and bake as usual.

■ Try using a coarse tea strainer instead of a flour sifter, when sprinkling **icing sugar** over small cakes.

Egg Substitutes in Cakes

■ When short of eggs for a cake mix, try a tablespoon of milk mixed with a level dessertspoon of custard powder.

■ Add a tablespoon of custard powder for every 500 g flour. Only 1 egg instead of three will be needed.

How to Bake Splendid Sponges

■ Sponge cakes will have a professional look if you first grease the tins, then sprinkle equal parts flour and caster sugar around them. This creates a delicious crust.

■ When making sponge cakes, break eggs on the sugar one hour before cooking begins, stirring them well with a fork. This melts the sugar, saves on beating time, and ensures a light sponge.

■ Try leaving out a teaspoon of flour from sponge cake mix, and substituting a teaspoon of arrowroot.

■ Delicious and light cakes: add two teaspoons of cold water to eggs and sugar mixture when making any sponge cake. Beating will be easier and the sponge will not sink.

■ Use a cotton thread to cut a sponge for filling.

■ See recipes under *Cooking*.

Storing Cakes

■ To store wedding cake, wrap the cake in cling wrap, put it in a plastic bag, and then freeze.

■ Place cake in a tightly sealed tin. The cake can be wrapped in aluminium foil first and the tin sealed with masking tape if you like.

■ Most cakes and biscuits stay fresher in a sealed bag in the fridge. Individually wrapped portions keep even better.

■ See also *Christmas Cakes*.

CAKE TINS
Rust Remedies

■ Sard Wonder Soap and steel wool will remove rust from cake tins.

■ Fill the cake tin with warm water and 1 teaspoon vinegar and stand overnight. Rust will wash off.

■ Next time you buy a cake tin, grease and heat it in oven for 15 minutes. It should never rust.

CAMPHORWOOD CHESTS

Allow Mr Sheen to soak in well before polishing and place camphor balls inside the chest. This will make your old chest look and smell like new.

CANDLES

To prevent candles dripping, chill them in the refrigerator for a few hours before lighting.

CANE
Cleaning Cane Furniture

■ Wash with warm soapy water. When dry, apply a little linseed oil.
■ Try washing cane with ¼ cup salt and 1 tablespoon of washing soda per litre of water, then dry and apply linseed oil.
■ It is a good idea to protect cane with a coat of clear shellac.

CANVAS

■ Canvas chairs can be **renovated** simply by stitching some new fabric over the canvas, and painting the arms.
■ To remove **mildew**, spread a mixture of soft soap, starch, salt and lemon juice over the canvas and leave in the sun. As it dries, apply more of mixture.
■ Do **not** apply household bleach to aged canvas, unless the stain is particularly bad. It is likely to destroy the fabric.
■ Commercial preparations are best for **waterproofing** canvas. Try Selleys Water Shield or Birkmyre Waterproofing Mixture.

CARDS

Cards may be cleaned by rubbing with talc, breadcrumbs or powdered magnesia. Don't use a rubber or art gum, as the cards become difficult to handle.

CARPETS

■ Remove **crush marks** from carpets caused by heavy furniture. Raise pile by pressing lightly with hot iron over a damp cloth or with a steam iron. Avoid excessive heat for synthetic carpets.
■ **Burn marks** on a carpet can be disguised by teasing the pile with steel wool. Work in a circular direction.
■ Carpets and upholstery can be cleansed of **grease-spots** with ammonia and water. Also helps freshen the colours.
■ To remove **chewing gum** from carpet or any article, Double D eucalyptus is excellent as it is a solvent. If gum is hard, several applications may be needed. Dab on the oil and leave to soften the gum. Remove as much as possible with knife blade and repeat process until all gum is removed. If any ring mark from the eucalyptus remains on the carpet, sponge off with warm water and Sunlight soap. Rinse with clean warm water and rub with a towel to dry.
■ Revive **colours** in carpets and rugs. Clean first, then wash over with a cloth wrung out in vinegar and water.
■ For **spilt wine** on a nylon carpet, sprinkle salt on the wine and when perfectly dry, vacuum. The stain will have disappeared, as the salt absorbs the moisture.
■ When you wash or clean a small area of carpet or upholstered furniture, use your blow drier (hold it at at least 30 cms away from the carpet) to remove excess moisture quickly. This **prevents rings.**

Make your own Carpet Soap

Shread 57 g of good washing soap. Pour over 1200 mls boiling water and store until dissolved. Add 3 tablespoons ammonia and 16 g washing soda. Store in screw top jars. To use, apply with cloth or brush to carpet and lather with hot water. Rinse out with cold water and dry off with clean cloth. About a tablespoon of this solution to 600 mls of water is adequate.

CARS
Hints for Buying a New Car

Think about these points before purchasing a new car.

■ **Interiors** should be cloth, not vinyl. It's cooler in summer and warmer in winter. Fabric should be treated with an approved sealer.

■ **Body style** should suit your needs. Families find four-doors and hatchbacks preferable to two-doors.

■ **Seats** should be positioned so that you don't have to stretch for anything, especially the pedals.

■ **Visibility** should be clear and unobstructed, without blind spots.

■ **The boot** must have enough space for your needs, and not be difficult to load and unload.

■ **Handling** should be smooth and direct, without excessive body roll. Make sure the car brakes in a straight line and has a good turning circle for ease of parking.

■ **Insurance** premiums differ between cars. Check to see if the premium for the car is within your budget.

Car Washing

Add ½ cup of kerosene to a bucket of cold water for washing. Allow to dry and polish with a soft cloth.

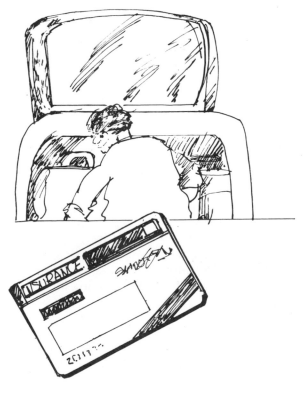

CASSEROLE

If you have broken the lid of your casserole, simply use aluminium foil as a cover.

■ See recipes under *Cooking*.

CAST IRON COOKWARE
New Cast Iron

When new, oil well using liquid vegetable oil. Make sure all the inside of the pan is well coated. Then heat for about 10 minutes on top of the stove on a low heat. Wipe off excess oil.

■ To keep your cast iron in good condition, after each use wash thoroughly in hot soap suds, rinse with boiling water and dry thoroughly. Then lightly oil. This is very important as cast iron cookware rusts easily and the oil prevents this from happening.

■ If your cast iron won't be used for a long time, rub thoroughly with oil or vaseline. Store in a very dry area and wash thoroughly before use.

Rust on Cast Iron Cookware

■ Rub the rust stains with dripping or oil then clean with steel wool soap pad. Wash in hot soapy water.

■ See also *Saucepans*.

CATS
Cat and Dog Repellants

■ Sprinkle napthalene flakes freely on the garden and between shrubs. This sure cure does not harm plants or grass. Buy the cheap type of flakes from the supermarket.

■ Chop, mash or grind a whole bulb (not just a clove) of garlic or a large strong onion. Add a tablespoon cayenne pepper or 1 teaspoon tabasco to 4 cups of tepid water. Let steep for 1 to 2 hours. Strain into sprayer or watering can. Use where needed.

■ A commercial preparation which is quite effective is Scent Off in an aerosol can.

CAULIFLOWER

Keep cauliflower white while cooking by either of these 2 methods. Either add 2 tablespoons of milk to the water while cooking, or add a pinch of baking powder in the same way.

CEREALS

Breakfast cereals that have gone soft may be crisped by leaving in a warm oven for 10 minutes. Allow to cool.

CHEESE

■ Mould can be prevented by storing cheese in a covered container with a lump or two of sugar. Also keeps cheese moist.
■ Slice cheese for salads with a potato peeler. Looks more attractive than conventional slices.

CHILBLAINS
Six Remedies for Chilblains

■ Mix equal parts castor oil and iodine, dab on with cotton wool, smooth onto affected parts. The castor oil softens swollen skin, prevents cracking and splitting. Iodine takes away the sting and itch of chilblains and prevents any infection if skin is already split.
■ Crush a cake of camphor and put into a small bottle. Add 1 tablespoon kerosene and leave to dissolve. Rub into inflamed parts as often as possible. After 1 or 2 days, chilblains will disappear completely.
■ Mix together equal parts of milk and turpentine, apply frequently to chilblains, but do not use on broken ones.
■ Take 1 tablespoon turpentine, DD Eucalyptus and methylated spirit or kerosene and the white of an egg and mix well. Apply for instant relief.

■ For relief from painful chilblains, rub the area with toothpaste.
■ You can also try applying half a teaspoon of bicarbonate of soda mixed with a teaspoon of vinegar.

CHOPS
Easy Sauces

■ Melt tablespoon butter in pan, add skinned and seeded tomato and cook for a few minutes. Add teaspoon curry powder and teaspoon flour, blended with a little milk, salt and pepper to taste. When thick, pour over grilled chops.
■ A little lemon juice squeezed over chops before cooking improves the flavour.

CHRISTMAS CAKES AND PUDDINGS

Handy Hints

■ Fruit cake may be moistened by piercing holes around the cake with a skewer. Every day for one week, pour quarter cup of sherry, brandy or other liquor over the cake. Store in an airtight container during and after treatment.

■ Roll dried fruits and nuts in cornflour before adding to mixture to stop them sinking to the bottom.

■ Leave Christmas cake upside down when cooling, to redistribute moisture.

■ Often a large Christmas cake is awkward to put into a cake tin. Place instead on a board covered with foil, then put into large plastic bag. Cake when required can be cut on the board.

■ Cut a double piece of brown paper a little bigger than the tin. Place this on top before putting in oven and the fruit cake will not burn on top.

■ Put four jam tins full of cold water in the oven when cooking the cake. The steam from the tins will keep the fruit cake moist during cooking.

■ Fruit cake will remain moist longer if half an apple is finely chopped and added with the fruit when mixing.

■ Another fruit cake tip: Your cake will not sink in the middle if you add the fruit before the flour.

■ See recipes under *Cooking*.

CHRISTMAS DECORATIONS

■ Here's a pretty idea for the **Christmas table**. Melt the bottoms of long red candles and stick to base of flower bowl. When firmly attached, fill bowl with water and float flowers in it.

■ Make small **Santa Clauses** from large toothpaste cartons. Cover with red paper and cottonwool head, red pipe cleaner arms and black paper belt. Paint faces. Great gift boxes for the kids.

■ Unusual candle holders for Christmas table: core bright red **apples**, place red candles in the holes. Place on table with flowers, green leaves and tinsel.

■ Melt old **candle** ends, using different colours if possible and pour them into pattycases. Stick small pieces of wick into the wax while it is setting. When wax is set, take from cases and float in a little water in a coloured bowl. The lighted candles look lovely for Christmas and the water reflects.

CHROME
Cleaning

■ Prevent rust by polishing with methylated spirits, then rub on petroleum jelly. Commercial preparations such as Incralac by Wattyl are also good.
■ For a fine shine rub on plain flour, then polish with a soft cloth.

CHUTNEY
Hints for Heavenly Chutney

Chop ingredients finely, add whole spices and seeds, in a muslin bag. Simmer with lid on pan until all ingredients soften. Long, slow cooking is important and may take from one to four hours. Stir thoroughly and often, and cook until the chutney is of the desired consistency. Put at once into hot clean jars and make airtight to prevent hardening and evaporation.
■ See recipes under *Cooking*.

CIRCULATION

This easy exercise improves circulation and is also good when feeling cold. Take at least 26 full deep breaths, hold as long as possible, let out as slowly as possible. Exercise your feet while seated. Point toes down as far as possible, then up and down at least 10 times.

CLEANING FLUID

Kerosene and vinegar (250 ml of each mixed together) make an excellent polish and cleaner for tiles, furniture, paint work, marble and lino.

CLOCKS

Try starting a clock or watch ticking again by placing a cloth sprinkled with kerosene over the open back. Leave overnight.

CLOTHES LINE

If you are short of clothes line space, peg socks to a wire coathanger, then peg hanger to the line.

CLOTHING

Prevent Clothes Clinging to Slips

Add fabric softener to final rinse. Also adds fresh softness to your wash.

Stiffening Lace Blouses

■ Buy 30 g gum arabic from chemist. Crush and wash gum, then soak until soft. Pour on 600 ml boiling water gradually, stirring until dissolved. Strain through muslin into a bottle and cork well. As a stiffening agent, use 1 tablespoon of the solution to a ½ litre of warm water.
■ Rinse in water to which methylated spirits has been added, 1 tablespoon to 5 litres of water. Press blouse while damp. Also good for curtains and crochet work.

Stiffening Synthetics

Gum Tragacanth is the perfect stiffener for unstarchable gear. Purchase from chemist and use 1 tablespoon to 600 ml warm water. Soak garment in liquid, do not wring but allow to drip dry, then press in usual way. The firmness will last from wash to wash.

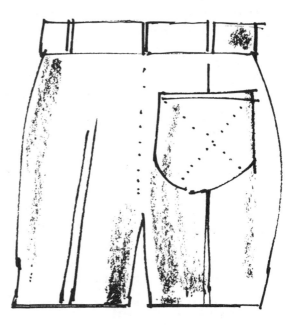

Softening Stiff Jeans

Dissolve 2 dessertspoons borax in 2½ litres of hot water. When cool, put the jeans in this mixture and leave until next day. Rinse in hot water, then wash in usual way.
■ Before washing jeans for the first time, soak for 24 hours in a strong solution of salt and hot water. Use 220 g salt to 1 bucket of hot water. Wash in normal way. Jeans never fade after this, nor do they run.

Revamping Worn Coats

When coats and jackets become worn around edges and button holes, buy a contrasting or matching coloured heavy duty seam binding or bias tape, and use to bind the edges.

Lurex Thread

■ Lurex thread is washable and does not tarnish. Wash the article according to the basic fibre. For instance, towels with lurex woven borders should be washed as cottons, and a wool stole with lurex threads should be washed as for wool.

23

Sensible Baby's Bibs

■ Attach elastic to baby's bibs, which saves having to tie the strings.
■ When making bibs for babies, line the underside with plastic to prevent milk or food soaking through to the clothes.

Stretching Short Overalls

If warm overalls shrink or have become too short for a child, knit cuffs in 1 purl, 1 plain, as you would for a jumper. Lengthen them with these. Sew to the bottom of the overalls' legs and they will give years more wear. They also provide more warmth.

Whitening Tennis Shorts

Spray new white tennis shorts with starch before wearing and after each cleaning. They will stay white longer.

Long-Lasting Socks

Before the socks are worn, darn with matching embroidery cotton, or any heavy thread, in places where toes do the damage.

Smooth Evening Dress Collars

Mix 30 g starch into 600 ml warm water. For really stiff articles, raw starching is easier and gives a better finish. Dip articles several times in starch solution. Work starch well into fabric. Wring heavily starched articles by hand. Hard wringing or extended spinning will reduce stiffness, so a little stronger starch solution may be needed in these cases. The stiffness obtained is controlled during ironing by extra dampening, the heat of the iron and the ironing pressure. To prevent sticking, avoid ironing wet articles. Gloss is achieved by applying pressure with a hot iron on an unpadded surface. A satin finish is achieved by touching with a damp cloth after ironing.

Masonic Aprons

■ Use Jif liquid cleaner on Masonic aprons.
Moisten a wad of cottonwool with water, squeeze on a little of the cleanser and rub gently over the soiled lambskin. Wipe over the treated area with clean damp cottonwool, then dry thoroughly. Apply a little colourless shoe cream, the kind used for leather shoes, and buff with a soft cloth. This will help preserve the soft lambskin. The linen or coarse grosgrain border on the apron is difficult to keep clean. Try diluted Wool Mix, half wool mix and half water. Apply with a stiff tooth brush, absorb any excess moisture with clean towelling. Note: Jif is a creamy liquid and cleanses without scratching.

Storing Clothes

■ Make sure cotton is thoroughly dry after washing to prevent the danger of **mildew** in storage.

■ Wrap **white cottons** and linens in blue tissue to stop yellowing and store clothing where strong light will not fade it.

■ Rinse **synthetic** fabrics in cool water to prevent wrinkles. Allow permanently-pleated fabrics to drip dry into shape before folding them for storage.

■ **Silk** should be kept in a cool, dry, dark place. Strong light can yellow silk or fade the dye.

■ Store suedes and **leather** in a cool, ventilated area, never in plastic bags.

■ Have proofing against **moths** and other insects in any area where clothing is stored.

■ **Tailored clothing** should be hung on well-padded, shaped hangers, not wire ones.

■ Do not crowd clothing hung in a closet. Leave space between hangers so garments can breathe and stay free of wrinkles.

■ Wrap a **christening robe** securely in blue acid free tissue paper, available at most newsagents and stationery shops. The paper will ensure the robe remains white. Then put in cardboard box with some moth balls or camphor. Make sure robe is clean before storing.

Clothing Stains and Smells

■ To clean raw meat fat or **fatty grease** from work overalls, put kerosene on the spots then peg them on the clothes line with grease spots facing the sun. Leave from early morning until sundown. Next day wash in warm water and soap. Then boil if they are white; if coloured wash and rinse in warm water and put on line to dry.

■ Here's another method of removing raw meat fat from overalls. Place 38 litres water in a copper, add 170 g to 225 g soap powder and ¾ cup of kerosene. Add the soiled clothes and boil for 30 minutes, stirring occasionally. Remove clothes and rinse once in hot water, then twice more in hot clear water to ensure that all greasy suds are removed.

■ Give **cricket ball** stains a good scrub with a cake of Solvol. Then wash trousers or shirts and hang in the sun with treated areas in direct sunlight. If not removed completely and garment is cotton or linen, soak in bleach for at least half an hour.

■ Dampen **grass stains** and rub area with methylated spirits or glycerine. Leave one hour, then wash as usual. Old stains will often come out if covered with glycerine. Wash out well. Soaking sports whites in Napisan not only removes grass stains but the garments stay a sparkling white. Solvol soap is also recommended.

■ It's possible to spruce up trousers with a **shiny seat**. Wipe shiny surface gently with a sponge wrung out in a solution of a cup of warm water and a dessertspoon white vinegar, then steam-press over a damp cloth. Repeat if necessary.

■ To remove **paint** on trousers, use white spirit. Soak the paint-stained part and keep scrubbing gently with an old nailbrush and rubbing by hand. The paint gradually softens but it's an effort, taking about 2 hours. However, all traces will eventually disappear with no damage to fabric.

■ Remove **paint** by saturating the spot 2 or 3 times with equal parts of turpentine and ammonia. Will remove paint even when dry and hard.

■ If **stained trousers** have not already been washed, try soaking them in warm water adding 2 tablespoons ammonia and 1 tablespoon vinegar in the water, plus 1 tablespoon salt. Leave overnight if possible. Rinse the next day in cold water and hang out to dry.

■ Methylated spirits dabbed on trousers also helps remove stains. However, you may be too late if trousers have already been washed.

■ To remove **perspiration odour** dissolve 2 heaped tablespoons bicarb of soda in ¾ bucketful cold or lukewarm water. Soak garments for 1 hour and then wash as usual. This is effective on all garments made from man-made fibre.

■ **Banana stains** can be conquered. Pour a little Sno-white bleach into its container top. Dip one finger into solution and apply to the stain. At first it will darken, but if you persevere, the stain will gradually disappear leaving fabric in good condition. Rinse very well.

■ Napisan is very good for removing banana stains and **sap** from white cotton athletic singlets. Dissolve powder in water as directed on packet, soak garment overnight. If stain persists, repeat treatment. As Napisan is a form of bleach use care with any coloured garment, but is excellent for whites. Napisan is obtainable from chemists.

■ Add 1 dessertspoon eucalyptus to soap powder in washing machine. This will remove oil and **oil smells**. If the oil persists, you may have to repeat the process.

■ Camphor is useful when there are **fruit stains** on tablecloths or clothing. Dampen camphor and rub over the stain, then wash as usual and stains will disappear.

■ Restore **yellowed clothing** by adding a teaspoon of turpentine to the water.

■ Before washing white socks, soak in salted water. Brown stains are then easily removed.

■ To whiten **baby clothes** buy a small can Dylon Super White from chemist. Follow instructions on can. Another remedy: soak yellowed clothes in water to which 1 packet of epsom salts has been added.

■ To whiten yellowed **bowls trousers** caused through dry cleaning and washing, try adding a teaspoon turpentine to the water and soak. Or cream of tartar restores whiteness to garments which cannot be bleached. Add 1 to 2 teaspoons to 4½ litres of hot water and soak overnight. A third option is to soak the trousers in a solution of 1 tablespoon borax to 500 ml water for 1 hour, then wash as usual, adding 1 tablespoon methylated spirits to the water.

■ **Yellowed woollens** can be rejuvenated with Rit Colour Remover. Available at chemists and haberdashery departments in stores.

COATHANGERS

Cover thin wooden coathangers with foam or put a piece at each end of the hanger. This will prevent clothes slipping off or becoming marked by hangers.

COCKROACHES
Cockroach Baits

■ Mix equal parts of powdered borax and sugar together. Place on plastic or metal lids in any cupboards or places where cockroaches are. This is supposed to keep houses cockroach-free for 3 months but has worked for up to 12 months, even in the tropics where roaches are prevalent.

■ Mix 4 tablespoons borax from chemist with 2 tablespoons plain flour or starch or sugar and 1 tablespoon cocoa. Leave out in upturned lids where cockroaches scuttle around. Note: keep children clear, as borax is poisonous.

■ Make a cockroach trap. Get a tall, wide-mouthed jar and smear inside with dripping for about half the length down from neck. Put a piece of bread or cake in the bottom. Roaches climb in, can't get out. Tip the trapped roaches into boiling water.

■ Put cucumber peelings into cupboards and around where roaches are found. Renew as peelings dry out.

COFFEE

To bring out flavour in coffee, put a pinch of salt in coffee grounds before water is added.

COINS

If your first instinct is to clean or polish old coins, don't. An expert will see what happened and will devalue the coin immediately. Once worn or polished away, the original sheen can never be restored. A coin should look its age. Only a proof or uncirculated coin which has not been coddled is expected to retain its original lustre. Coins which tone gracefully are often more desirable than those with shiny surface.

COLDS
Preventing or Minimising

■ Dress properly for cold weather and make sure you are not over-exposed to either heat or cold.

■ Eat sensibly. Try to stick to a balanced diet that includes vitamins, protein and nutrients, from the four major food groups: meat and fish, dairy products, vegetables and grains, and fruits. Avoid fad or starvation diets that can lower your resistance.

■ Stay away from places where you know people have the flu. It is an air-borne disease, so if you see people wheezing and sneezing, avoid them. Don't socialise with friends if they have colds or flu.

■ If you work among groups of people at high risk from the disease, get a flu vaccination. These groups include people over 65 and those with underlying chronic illness including heart, kidney and respiratory disease, diabetes and conditions that lower the body's resistance.

■ Don't share cups or spoons with someone else. If a member of the family is sick, make sure that used tissues are frequently removed.

■ Proper exercise can help ward off reactions to bad colds and viruses. But use common sense. Don't start a vigorous exercise program or run 10 kilometres if it's freezing cold outside.

■ Go to bed as soon as you recognise the early signs of a cold or flu. If you have a fever or cough, don't go to work or school. Stay home and take care of yourself. Your cold will improve by leaps and bounds but you won't improve if you try to keep your normal schedule.

■ Stay in bed until your fever has gone for 24 hours, you are eating normally and you feel better. If you get up and feel washed out, get back into bed and wait until you get your strength back.

■ Drink plenty of water and juices and take aspirin according to the directions on the bottle.

■ If you have a fever for more than three days, have a cough and phlegm for more than 24 hours, develop shortness of breath because of chest congestion, have diarrhoea for more than 48 hours, cannot take fluids because of nausea or have blood in your stools, you should always see your doctor right away.

COOKING

The following recipes are just a small collection of those which have appeared in Molly Dye's column over the years. In each case these recipes have proved to be family favourites, with readers constantly requesting that the recipe be repeated, so that once again they could add it to their prized recipe collection.

MEAT AND SEAFOOD
Paradise Casserole

1 kg chuck or blade steaks cut into 5 cm cubes
½ teaspoon ground ginger
2 tablespoons flour
1 teaspoon salt
pepper
2 tablespoons oil
2 sticks diced celery
3 sliced onions
1 cup beef stock
⅓ cup vinegar
465 g can tomatoes, drained
½ cup brown sugar
6 carrots, sliced diagonally
465 g can crushed pineapple, drained
½ cup raisins soaked in ½ cup pineapple liquid

Toss steak in flour and ginger. Brown in heated oil. Remove steak from pan. Sauté celery and onion for a few minutes. Replace steak, add stock, vinegar, tomatoes, sugar, salt and pepper. Cover and cook over moderate heat until tender, about 2 hours. During last 30 minutes add carrots, pineapple and raisins.

Toad in the Hole

500 g sausages
knob of dripping
125 g plain flour
pinch salt
1 egg
300 mL milk

Sift flour and salt. Drop in egg and beat well. Gradually beat in enough milk to make a stiff smooth batter. Let stand for a few minutes. Beat in the rest of the milk. Put the sausages and dripping into an ovenproof dish. Cook for 10 minutes in a hot oven. Pour in the batter and return to a very hot oven for 30 minutes.

Lemon Sauce Pork

4 pieces fillet pork, flattened and cut into
    serving pieces
1 egg
seasoned flour
125 g butter

Dip fillets into beaten egg then toss in seasoned flour. Melt 60 g butter in frying pan and when it starts to sizzle add pork fillets. Cook for a few minutes on both sides, add rest of butter and cook for a further 8 to 10 minutes. Serve with lemon sauce, sliced mushrooms and small potatoes.

Lemon sauce:
1 tablespoon cornflour
1 cup water
pinch salt
2 shallot stalks, chopped
½ red capsicum, cut in strips
1 teaspoon grated lemon rind
3 tablespoons lemon juice
1 tablespoon butter

Blend cornflour smoothly with water and salt. Bring to boil, stirring constantly and cook for 3 minutes over low heat. Add shallots, capsicum, lemon rind, juice and butter and whisk well before serving and garnish with shredded lemon rind.

Veal Parmigiana

500 g veal steak, 4 slices
30 g grated Parmesan cheese
30 g breadcrumbs
pinch each pepper and salt
1 egg, lightly beaten
60 g butter
250 g peeled ripe tomato pulp
pinch oregano
pinch sugar
pinch onion salt
125 g mozzarella cheese

Mix together Parmesan, breadcrumbs, pepper and salt. Dip veal steaks in beaten egg, then in breadcrumb mixture. Melt butter in baking dish (large enough to hold the four steaks) then add steaks. Bake in pre-heated oven at 200°C for 15 to 20 minutes. Turn meat over and continue baking for another 15 minutes. In saucepan, bring to boil the tomatoes, oregano, onion salt and sugar, stirring constantly. When meat is ready, pour sauce over and top with slices of mozzarella cheese. Return to oven for 2 to 3 minutes until cheese melts.

Corned Beef Hash

2 cups diced cold boiled potatoes
1½ cups chopped corned beef
1 small onion, minced
⅜ cup cream
3 tablespoons butter
salt and pepper
paprika
6 eggs

Combine potatoes, corned beef and onion. Add ¼ cup cream and 1 tablespoon melted butter. Season and mix well. Place mixture in buttered baking dish. With bottom of a custard cup, make 6 indentations in the hash and dot each with bits of butter, using 1 tablespoon in all. Bake in a very hot oven 230°C for 15 minutes. Remove from oven and into each indentation break one egg, and dot with the remaining butter. Bake in moderate oven 180°C until the eggs are set, 15 to 20 minutes.

Good Old Chicken Stew

1 boiling fowl
90 g bacon
1 large onion
60 g diced mixed root vegetables
liquid seasoning
salt and pepper
600 mL water
30 g flour
150 mL milk
chopped parsley

Wash chicken in cold water. Cut into 8 neat pieces, 2 joints from each leg, 2 from breast and wings. Dice bacon and put into pan with chopped onion, vegetables and chicken. Add seasonings and water. Put on lid, simmer gently for 2–2¼ hours until chicken is tender. If using young chicken, allow only a little more than 1 hour. Blend flour with milk, stir into liquid. Bring to boil, stirring well and cook until smooth and thickened. Taste, add more seasoning if necessary. Garnish with chopped parsley.

Duck with Orange

1 × 2.5–3 kg duck
coarse salt
1 whole orange
1 clove garlic
2 bay leaves
1 cup red wine
½ large onion, finely chopped
125 g mushrooms (finely chopped)
3 dessertspoons duck fat
3 teaspoons potato flour or plain flour
½ teaspoon tomato paste
1 teaspoon beef extract
1 cup stock
2 teaspoons shredded orange rind
skinned sections from 2 oranges
¼ cup brandy
salt and pepper

Rub duck well with coarse salt. Stuff with the orange, cut in quarters, garlic and bay leaves. Tie up, roast in hot oven 1 to 1¼

hours. Baste about every 15 minutes with red wine, using half cup in all. Meanwhile make sauce. Sauté duck liver, onion and mushrooms in 2 dessertspoons duck fat from the roasting pan. Remove liver, add another dessertspoon fat. Remove from heat. Blend in flour, tomato paste and beef extract. Add stock and remainder of wine. Stir over heat until it comes to the boil. Add orange rind and season to taste. Simmer until duck is ready to serve (be careful not to burn). Just before serving add skinned orange sections.

To serve cut duck into serving pieces, arrange down centre of hot platter. If potatoes are being served, pile at one end. Skim fat off pan juices, pour in brandy and bring to boil to dissolve beef extract. Pour this into the orange sauce. Spoon a little over the duck. A few orange sections can be reserved to arrange on each side of dish with the sautéed liver. Serve remainder of sauce in heated gravy boat.

Macaroni Tuna

125 g macaroni, cooked
215 g can tuna
1 tablespoon butter
¼ cup chopped celery
¼ cup chopped onion
310 g can tomato soup (undiluted)
pepper to taste
½ cup grated cheese

Drain and flake tuna. Melt butter in saucepan, add celery and onion and cook until soft. Add soup and pepper, simmer gently for about 15 minutes. Arrange layers of cooked macaroni, tuna and sauce into greased casserole dish covering each layer of sauce with cheese. Bake uncovered in moderate oven until sauce bubbles, about 30 minutes.

Baked Whole Fish

1 whole bream or flathead or snapper
lemon juice
1 cup soft white breadcrumbs
salt and pepper

sprinkle of nutmeg
2 level tablespoons chopped parsley
1 level tablespoon butter
¼ cup milk
lemon and parsley to garnish

Thoroughly wipe fish which has been cleaned first. Cut off fins and trim tail (using scissors), remove eyes. Rub inside and outside of fish with lemon juice. Mix breadcrumbs with a little salt, pepper, nutmeg, chopped parsley, and about half the butter. Place about half this mixture inside fish. Fasten fish together with skewers or sew. Do not over-fill as breadcrumb seasoning swells in cooking. Grease ovenproof dish or baking dish, place fish in. Brush with milk to prevent drying out. Cover with remaining seasoning and dot with butter. Cover with greased paper; the addition of about ¼ cup milk will prevent excessive drying. Bake in moderate oven, 190°C–200°C for 20 to 30 minutes depending on size and thickness. The fish is cooked if tender when tested with skewer. Test in thickest part. The quantity of butter given in the recipe is sufficient for baking purposes.

Ginger Prawns

750 g cooked prawns
4 tablespoons water
1 chicken stock cube
1 tablespoon oil
2 teaspoons grated green ginger
1 dessertspoon finely chopped onion
1 tablespoon white wine
1 teaspoon soy sauce

Shell prawns, leaving tails on and remove black vein. Combine water and crumbled stock cube. Heat oil, fry ginger and onion for 2 minutes. Add wine, chicken stock and soy sauce, bring to boil. Add prawns, heat through gently about 2 minutes over low heat. Drain and serve with saffron rice.

Scallops Mornay

1 cup dry wine
1 small onion
3 peppercorns
60 g butter or margarine
½ cup flour
300 mL milk
salt
pepper
pinch nutmeg
¼ teaspoon dry mustard
60 g cheese
45 g butter or margarine
6 shallots
1 kg scallops
½ cup sour cream
½ cup cream
30 g butter or margarine, extra
1 cup fresh breadcrumbs
60 g cheese, extra

Put wine in saucepan with peeled and sliced onion and peppercorns, bring slowly to boil. Reduce heat, simmer until liquid is reduced by half. Strain and reserve. Melt butter, add flour, stir over low heat 1 minute. Gradually add milk and reserved liquid, stir until sauce boils and thickens. Reduce heat, simmer 2 minutes. Remove from heat, season with salt and pepper. Add nutmeg, mustard and grated cheese, stir until cheese melts. Melt extra 45 g butter in pan, add finely chopped shallots. Wash and trim scallops, dry well. Add to pan, sauté gently over low heat until just cooked, about 7 minutes.

Add to hot sauce with sour cream, then stir in cream. Put in greased ovenproof dishes or 6 small scallop shells. Melt remaining butter, remove from heat, add breadcrumbs, toss lightly; add extra grated cheese, sprinkle over top of scallops. Heat under griller to brown crumbs lightly. Serves 4 as main course or 6 as an entrée.

Crisp Batter

¼ cup full cream powdered milk
½ cup self-raising flour
1½ cups plain flour
1 teaspoon salt
¼ teaspoon pepper
1½ cups water

Sift dry ingredients into a mixing bowl and make a well in the middle. Gradually stir in the water and mix to a smooth batter. Deep fry your coated meat or fish in hot oil until golden brown. Drain thoroughly.

VEGETABLES

Zucchini Salad

500 g zucchini
250 g macaroni
2 medium white onions
1 medium green capsicum
1 tablespoon chopped parsley
1 dessertspoon chopped chives
1 tin red kidney beans
salt and pepper
1 tablespoon Italian dressing
1 dessertspoon white vinegar
1 tablespoon mayonnaise

Cook macaroni in boiling salted water and allow to cool. Cut zucchini into quarters and then slice. Cover with boiling water and half teaspoon salt. Leave for a few minutes. Drain and cool. Chop onions and capsicum, add to macaroni and zucchini, with the parsley, chives and drained beans. Season with salt and pepper to taste. Mix Italian dressing (bought variety) and vinegar and mayonnaise, well together. Fold through mixture and put in fridge to cool.

Bubble and Squeak

leftover vegetables, such as cabbage, peas, beans, etc.
leftover potatoes
butter
salt and pepper

Put potatoes and vegetables in mixing bowl. Mash together with a little butter, salt and pepper. Melt a little butter in frying pan. Spread mashed vegetables in pan and fry gently until one side is golden crisp. Turn over by putting a plate in pan, inverting then sliding mixture back into pan (mixture should be about 2.5 cm deep). Fry till under side is also crisp, so that both sides form a firm, golden crust. Slide bubble and squeak onto serving dish and serve by cutting into cake-shape slices. Can also be served cold with salad. Preparation and cooking time amounts to approximately 10 minutes.

Pumpkin Cheese

1 kg cooked pumpkin
2 tablespoons butter
½ cup cooked rice
pepper and salt
1 cup milk
2 eggs
60 g cheese
30 g extra cheese
paprika

Mash pumpkin with rice, butter, seasonings and milk. Beat eggs, add to pumpkin with cheese. Place in ovenware dish, sprinkle with extra cheese and paprika, also breadcrumbs if liked, and bake at 180°C until brown, about 20 minutes.

Baked Corn with Capsicums

2 cups canned corn niblets
¾ cup soft breadcrumbs
2 tablespoons butter
1 egg
½ cup cream
1–3 cups finely chopped capsicum
1 teaspoon Worcestershire sauce
½ teaspoon salt
⅛ teaspoon pepper

Mix well together. Turn into greased casserole. Bake in moderate oven 180°C for 20 minutes.

Potato Scallops

500 g potatoes
boiling water
2 cups flour
1 egg
1 tablespoon oil
1–1½ cups hot water
¼ teaspoon salt
oil for deep frying

Peel potatoes and wash well. Cut into slices 6 mm thick. Put into heatproof basin and cover with boiling water. Stand for 1 hour. Meanwhile prepare batter, sift flour and salt into basin. Make a well in the centre and add beaten egg and oil, beat in enough hot water to make a fairly thick coating batter. Beat until smooth. Drain potatoes and pat dry. Coat each slice well with batter. Deep fry in hot oil, a few at a time, until batter is golden brown and crisp. Drain on kitchen paper and sprinkle with salt.

Onion Rings

3 large white onions
½ cup flour
¾ teaspoon salt
pepper
½ teaspoon baking powder
1 well-beaten egg
½ cup milk
little cooking oil

Wash and peel onions, cut into 6 mm slices. Separate into rings. Mix flour, seasonings and baking powder together and add mixture of the egg and milk. Blend thoroughly. Dip rings in batter, drop into deep fat heated to 185°C. Fry until golden brown. Drain on absorbent paper and sprinkle with salt.

DESSERTS
Chocolate Pudding

125 g grated chocolate
125 g breadcrumbs
125 g sugar
60 g butter, melted
4 eggs

Mix all ingredients together well, add eggs and stir well with a fork for 10 minutes, put in a mould and steam 1½ hours.

Sauce:

125 g grated chocolate
60 g moist sugar
300 mL milk
a little vanilla

Place all ingredients in saucepan, boil for a few minutes and pour over pudding.

Wine Trifle

1 sponge, cooked in Swiss roll tin
120 mL wine, sherry or port
4 bananas, sliced and sprinkled with lemon
    juice
maraschino cherries (optional)
450 mL boiling water
1 packet lemon or port wine jelly

Custard:

300 mL milk
2 eggs
125 g sugar
1 teaspoon vanilla
1 dessertspoon gelatine
1 tablespoon water
whipped cream
toasted chopped almonds

Cut sponge into fingers, brush with wine, place around sides of spring form pan. Cut remaining sponge into triangles, place around base of tin, sprinkle with remaining wine. Arrange some of the banana on base. Make jelly and allow to partly set, pour a small amount over sponge and fruit base.

Set in refrigerator. Combine remaining jelly and banana, pour over base. Set in refrigerator. Beat eggs and sugar, place in double boiler with milk, vanilla and gelatine softened in water. Cook, stirring until thick, cool, then pour over jelly and allow to set until firm. Unmould carefully, tie with narrow ribbon. Decorate with cream, nuts and cherries.

Bread and Butter Pudding

3 slices stale bread
a little butter
2 eggs, separated
1 tablespoon sugar
2 cups milk
a little lemon rind
1 tablespoon jam
2 sliced bananas (optional)
1 tablespoon caster sugar

Butter bread, remove crusts, and cut into fingers. Place in a greased pie dish. Beat together well the egg yolks, sugar, milk and lemon rind. Pour mixture over the bread. Bake in slow oven, 160°C for about an hour or until set. Do not let the pudding boil, slow baking is necessary. When the pudding is baked, spread with the jam and bananas. Beat the egg whites until stiff and sprinkle over the caster sugar. Beat well. Spoon meringue on top of the pudding and return to oven until meringue is golden.

Peach Cobbler

6–8 medium sized peaches
1 cup sugar
1 level tablespoon cornflour
pinch salt
finely grated rind 1 lemon
1 tablespoon lemon juice
few drops almond essence
1 tablespoon butter

Topping:
1½ cups self-raising flour
pinch salt
¼ cup sugar
90 g butter or margarine

1 egg, beaten
½ cup milk
1 level teaspoon caster sugar
2 level teaspoons cinnamon

Peel and slice peaches, mix sugar, cornflour, salt and lemon rind, add to peaches and fold through. Sprinkle with lemon juice and almond essence. Empty into a greased large shallow type ovenproof dish, put in moderate oven and cook until hot and bubbling, about 15 minutes. Prepare topping while peaches are cooking. Sift flour, salt, sugar, rub in butter lightly, add milk to beaten egg, add to dry ingredients, making scone type dough. Drop into hot bubbling mixture when it is removed from oven. Return to moderately hot oven, bake until cooked and browned, about 30 minutes. Serve while still hot with whipped cream, custard or ice cream.

Strawberry Chiffon Pie

1 punnet strawberries, washed & hulled
5 tablespoons caster sugar
1½ tablespoons gelatine
2 tablespoons cold water
3 eggs, separated
1 cup cream
½ teaspoon vanilla essence
20 cm crumb crust

Place strawberries, sugar and one tablespoon water into a saucepan. Heat gently until sugar dissolves then bring to a rapid boil for 2 minutes. Remove from heat and purée. Return to saucepan and whisk in the beaten yolks. Stir over low heat until mixture thickens slightly. Remove from heat and pour into a bowl. Cool slightly.

Dissolve gelatine with cold water over hot water and combine with thickened strawberry mixture. Cool until partially set.

Whisk whites until soft peaks form, gently fold into strawberry mixture. Whip cream with vanilla until thick and fold in. Spoon mixture into prepared crust and refrigerate until firm.

Decorate with extra cream and strawberries if desired.

Economical Two-Egg Pavlova

2 egg whites
1½ cups castor sugar
½ teaspoon vanilla
1 teaspoon each white vinegar and
   cornflour
4 tablespoons boiling water
Place all ingredients in small bowl of
electric mixer. Beat on low speed until
mixture starts to thicken, then high speed
until mixture is very stiff, about 15
minutes. Spread on to a foil-lined tray. This
mixture makes a 28 cm pavlova or 15
small shells. Put the pavlovas in a moderate
oven at 150°C for 10 minutes, then reduce
to slow, 90°C, and bake another 45
minutes. For shells: cook 10 minutes at
150°C then 30 minutes at 95°C. For both;
cool in oven with door slightly open.

Custard Tart

Biscuit pastry:
90 g butter
¼ cup sugar
1 egg
1¼ cups plain flour
¼ cup self-raising flour

Filling:
3 eggs
1 teaspoon vanilla
2 tablespoons sugar
2 tablespoons full cream powdered milk
2¼ cups warm milk
nutmeg

   Pastry — Beat butter until creamy, add
sugar, mix until just combined. Add beaten
egg gradually, beat in well. Work in sifted
flours with a wooden spoon. Knead lightly
to form a smooth shape. Refrigerate for 30
minutes before using. Roll pastry on a
lightly floured board. Carefully line a well
greased 20 cm tart plate. Pinch the edges
decoratively.
   Filling — Beat eggs, vanilla and sugar
together. Blend the powdered milk into the
warm milk. Gradually stir into the egg
mixture.

Carefully spoon the custard mixture into
the pastry case. Bake in a 175°C oven for
30–35 minutes. After 15 minutes of
cooking time, sprinkle the tart with nutmeg.

Low Sugar Pudding

½ cup sultanas
½ cup raisins
½ cup currants
¼ cup mixed peel
¼ cup washed glace cherries
½ teaspoon ground cinnamon
pinch nutmeg and ground cloves
½ cup water
1 cup self-raising wholemeal flour
¼ cup skimmed milk
1 egg white, unbeaten
Line a steam pudding basin with foil. Place
fruit, spices and water in a saucepan,
simmer 3 minutes, cool. Add flour, milk
and egg white to fruit mixture. Stir well.
Pour into basin and cover tightly; steam for
1 hour. For extra flavour, a little dry sherry
may be added after the fruit has cooled.

Leftover Cake Dessert

Crumbled cake
4 tablespoons honey
3 eggs
2 cups milk
1 dessertspoon sugar
Butter a medium sized pie dish, fill with
crumbled cake and spread with half the
honey. Beat the eggs, reserving the whites
of 2. Pour the mixture over the cake
crumbs and stand dish in a baking dish of
cold water. Bake in a fairly hot oven until
set, about half an hour. Whip eggs stiffly,
add a little sugar. When pudding is set,
spread the remaining honey on top, then
pile beaten egg whites on top, and return to
cool part of oven to brown slightly. Serve
with whipped cream.

Light and Fluffy Pancakes

1 cup self-raising flour
pinch salt
¼ teaspoon bicarbonate soda
3 tablespoons sugar
1 egg beaten
½ cup sour milk
1 dessertspoon melted butter

Sift dry ingredients into basin, add sugar. Mix to smooth batter with beaten egg and milk, add melted butter. Heat and grease pan, drop batter by dessertspoonfuls on to pan, cook until bubbly on top, light brown underneath. Turn and cook other side.

CAKES AND BISCUITS
Special Sponge Cake

4 large eggs or 5 small eggs
185 g caster sugar
pinch salt
1 cup self-raising flour
1 level tablespoon butter
3 tablespoons ½ milk, ½ water which
  must be boiling when added to mixture

Separate eggs, being careful not to break yolk into white. Add salt to whites. Beat whites until just taking shape, then gradually add sugar, about a tablespoon each addition until all is added and the mixture is well mixed but not too stiff. Then add egg yolks one at a time, do not overbeat, just blend in. Sift self-raising flour twice and add by sifting into egg and sugar mixture, immediately fold in flour very lightly, do not beat. Then add butter, milk and water mixture which is at boiling point. Make sure liquid is evenly stirred, not beaten, into mixture. Have two 20 cm sandwich tins ready which have been greased with hot dripping, drain excess off and when set, dust with self-raising flour. Put mixture into prepared tins and cook for 20 minutes in oven set at 200°C on middle shelf. Turn out of tins immediately when cooked.

German Coffee Cake

125 g butter or substitute
½ cup caster sugar
3 eggs
½ teaspoon vanilla essence
2 cups self-raising flour
pinch salt
½ cup milk

Topping:
30 g butter or substitute
1 tablespoon brown sugar
1 tablespoon coconut
¼ cup plain flour
1 tablespoon chopped glacé cherries
1 tablespoon chopped walnuts

Cream butter and sugar until light and fluffy. Add vanilla, beat in eggs one at a time, beat well. Mix in sifted flour and salt alternately with milk. Pour into well greased loaf tin.

Topping:
Cream butter, sugar and flour. Press this topping through coarse sieve over top of cake. Mix together coconut, cherries and walnuts. Sprinkle on, press down lightly with fingers. Bake in moderate oven 50 minutes. Cool in tin 10 minutes, turn on to folded tea towel on wire rack. Note: to prevent topping breaking, invert at once.

Banana Cake

100 g butter or margarine
½ cup sugar
1 egg
½ cup plain flour
1 cup self-raising flour
pinch salt
vanilla essence

Filling:
½ cup chopped dates
1 dessertspoon lemon juice
1 large banana, mashed

To prepare filling heat gently the dates and lemon juice until nice and soft. Beat in mashed banana. Cream butter and sugar until nice and fluffy. Add egg and vanilla, beat well. Mix in sifted flours and salt. Spread half the mixture in greased and floured 20 cm cake pan. Top with date filling, spread as evenly as possible remaining cake mixture on top. Bake in moderate oven 25 to 30 minutes. When cold, dust with icing sugar.

Eggless chocolate cake

125 g butter
⅔ cup caster sugar
1 teaspoon vanilla
2 tablespoons golden syrup
1½ cups milk
1 teaspoon bicarbonate of soda
2½ cups self-raising flour
3 tablespoons cocoa
Sift together flour and cocoa. Cream butter and sugar until light and fluffy. Stir in vanilla and golden syrup, beat well. Fold in sifted dry ingredients with the milk making a soft consistency. Butter and line 2 sandwich pans. Bake on centre shelf of 180°C (350°F) oven for 30 to 35 minutes. When cold, sandwich together with a lemon filling.

Three-Minute Cake

1 cup flour
⅔ cup sugar
3 eggs
2 tablespoons butter
2½ tablespoons milk
1 teaspoon cream of tartar
½ teaspoon soda
With wooden spoon beat together all the ingredients except the tartar and soda. Add these when the mixture is smooth. Bake in moderate oven for about 15 minutes.

Rocky Road Frosting

30 g butter
3 tablespoons cold water
1 teaspoon coffee powder
2½ cups icing sugar plus
3 tablespoons cocoa sifted together
125 g marshmallows, chopped
3 tablespoons toasted desiccated coconut
3 tablespoons unsalted peanuts, chopped
½ cup popcorn
Melt butter, add water, coffee, sifted ingredients and beat until smooth. Mix in marshmallows, coconut, peanuts and popcorn. Pour over top and sides of cake.

Mock cream

1 level tablespoon cornflour
30 g sugar
150 ml milk
30 g copha
pinch salt
vanilla essence
Blend cornflour with a little of the milk, place remaining milk and salt on to boil. Stir in blended cornflour and boil for 2 minutes, stirring constantly. Set aside to cool. Soften copha at room temperature and gradually add sugar, beating until dissolved. Beat in vanilla and cornflour mixture gradually, about a dessertspoon at a time and continue beating until smooth and creamy.

Lamingtons

175 g butter
¾ cup caster sugar
3 eggs, beaten
2 cups self-raising flour
150 mL milk
½ teaspoon vanilla essence

Icing:
25 g butter
¼ cup boiling water
2 tablespoons cocoa
2 cups icing sugar
2 cups desiccated coconut

Two days before you make lamingtons, make the cake. Preheat oven to 180°C (350°F). Grease a Swiss roll tin, line it with greaseproof paper and re-grease.

Cream butter and sugar until light and fluffy. Gradually add eggs, beating well after each addition. Alternately fold in flour and milk, stir in vanilla essence.

Place mixture in greased, lined Swiss roll tin and bake for 30–35 minutes. Cool cake on wire rack.

To make lamingtons, cut cake into 3.5 cm cubes.

Prepare icing: place butter in a bowl and pour in boiling water. Add cocoa and, beating continuously, gradually add icing sugar. Place bowl of icing over pan of hot water. Using a long pronged fork to hold cubes of cake, dip each piece into icing and roll immediately in coconut. Leave lamingtons to set. Makes approximately 12.

Date Slice

Biscuit Pastry: Sufficient to line and cover a lamington tin.

1 egg
½ cup caster sugar
¼ cup butter
1 tablespoon lemon juice
2½ cups plain flour
1 level teaspoon baking powder
pinch salt

Beat egg and sugar till thick. Add butter and lemon juice, beat in well. Add sifted dry ingredients. Turn on to floured surface and knead lightly. Divide into two-third and one-third portions. Roll out the two-third portion to line a greased lamington tin. Spread date mixture over pastry. Roll out remaining pastry to cover date mixture. Glaze lightly with water, sprinkle with sugar. Bake in moderate oven (190°–200°C) for 30 to 35 minutes till golden; allow to cool slightly in tin.

Date Mixture:

2 cups dates
4 tablespoons warm water
3 tablespoons lemon or orange juice
grated rind ½ lemon or ½ orange

Chop dates, place in saucepan with remaining ingredients. Cook till thick and smooth. Allow to cool. Note: slice may be iced while warm if desired.

Ginger Crunch Biscuits

125 g butter
125 g caster sugar
215 g plain flour
1 teaspoon baking powder
1 teaspoon ground ginger

Icing:

30 g butter
60 g icing sugar
2 teaspoons golden syrup
1 teaspoon ground ginger

Cream butter and sugar. Add sifted dry ingredients. Mix well and press into greased 20 cm square tin. Bake in moderate oven 160°C for 25–30 minutes. Put butter, icing sugar, golden syrup and ground ginger in saucepan. Heat over low heat until melted, then pour over biscuits while hot. Cut into slices while still warm.

CHRISTMAS DELIGHTS
Christmas Pudding

500 g seeded raisins
250 g sultanas
250 g currants
250 g flour
2 level teaspoons mixed spice
2 level teaspoons powdered nutmeg
½ teaspoon salt
250 g soft white breadcrumbs
500 g beef suet
250 g stoned dates
250 g figs
250 g mixed peel
250 g sugar
90 g blanched almonds
6 eggs
300 mL milk
1 teaspoon almond essence
150 mL brandy or rum

Sift together flour, spices and salt. Skin and shred the suet very finely with the flour, blanch and chop the almonds. Chop the fruit finely, washing the peel to remove the sugar. If desired the fruit may be soaked in the rum or brandy for some hours before adding to cake mixture. Mix all dry ingredients thoroughly, then stir in the beaten eggs and milk. Mix well. Add brandy and essence and blend well into mixture. Grease basin well and two-thirds fill with the pudding mixture, cover with thick buttered paper and tie securely. Stand on a rack in a big boiler or saucepan with enough water to come half way up the sides of the basin and boil for 4 hours. Keep the water boiling round the basin, and keep a kettle of water boiling ready to fill it up as the water boils away. Be careful the water does not bubble up over the top of the basin or the puddings will be soggy. Steam for 4 hours on day of making then reheat for about an hour on serving. Serve with hard sauce or brandy sauce as you prefer.

Fruit Mince

60 g currants
60 g raisins
60 g sultanas
2 apples
125 g brown sugar
30 g lemon peel
rind and juice of 1 lemon
½ teaspoon mixed spice
1 tablespoon sherry

Peel and core apples, mince all ingredients together, add sugar, spice, lemon juice and sherry. Let stand for at least one hour before using. May be made days before and stored in the refrigerator.

White Christmas Candy

250 g white vegetable shortening
3 cups rice bubbles
1 cup coconut
¾ cup icing sugar
1 cup powdered milk
¼ cup chopped mixed peel
¼ cup preserved ginger
¼ cup glacé apricots
¼ cup glacé pineapple
¼ cup sultanas
¼ cup chopped glacé cherries

Melt chopped white vegetable shortening over gentle heat and allow to cool. Combine rice bubbles, coconut, sifted icing sugar, powdered milk and chopped fruits. Mix well. Add shortening and mix thoroughly. Press mixture into lightly greased and paper-lined lamington tin. Refrigerate until firm, cut into bars for serving.

Jellied Christmas Pudding

250 g raisins
500 g sultanas
125 g currants
60 g mixed peel
¾ cup sugar
2 cups water
60 g glacé cherries
60 g glacé apricots
60 g toasted slivered almonds
1–1⅓ cups water, extra
3½ tablespoons gelatine
1 cup sweet sherry
¼ cup brandy
¼ cup lemon juice
30 g glacé cherries, extra

Chop raisins finely; combine with sultanas, currants and mixed peel. Wash thoroughly, drain. It may be necessary to wash fruit several times so that it is completely clean; this will ensure a beautifully clear jellied pudding. Combine fruit, sugar and water in saucepan, stir over low heat until sugar is dissolved; increase heat slightly, simmer uncovered 10 minutes. Drain, reserve liquid, strain liquid through fine cloth. Place fruit and strained liquid into large basin, add finely chopped glacé cherries and apricots. Add gelatine to extra water, stand 5 minutes, dissolve over hot water, add to fruit mixture. Add almonds, sherry, brandy and lemon juice, mix well. Take ⅓ cup liquid from fruit mixture, pour half over base of oiled 20 cm baba tin or 2 litre mould; refrigerate until partly set. Quarter extra cherries, arrange decoratively in jelly, pour over remaining liquid. Refrigerate until set. Top with fruit mixture, refrigerate overnight. Unmould carefully. Note: This pudding is best eaten within 3 days of making.

A No-Bake Christmas Cake

125 g copha
250 g milk coffee biscuits
90 g brown sugar
½ teaspoon salt
1 tablespoon cocoa
1 teaspoon mixed spice
125 g chopped dates
45 g chopped raisins
30 g chopped mixed nuts
grated rind 1 orange
3 tablespoons sherry or orange juice
1 tablespoon coffee essence
Melt copha over low heat. Crush biscuits and place in large mixing bowl with sugar, salt, cocoa, spice, fruit, nuts and orange rind. Combine sherry and coffee essence with melted copha, add to dry ingredients and mix thoroughly. Press mixture into 15 cm round or 17 cm square lined cake tin. Place in fridge until set. Serve in small blocks. Store in fridge.

Easiest-Ever Christmas Cake

1 cup water
113 g butter
1 cup brown sugar
1 cup each currants, sultanas and dates or raisins
1 teaspoon spice
1 level teaspoon carb soda
1 cup self-raising flour
1 cup flour
2 eggs
Boil together the water, butter, sugar and fruit for 10 minutes. Allow to cool, then add the beaten eggs and flour sifted with the soda and spice. Turn into prepared tin and bake about 1¼ to 1½ hours at 200°C. Place a layer of foil or brown paper loosely over top of cake tin for the last half of cooking time.

Plastic icing

This icing will cover a 20 × 20 cm or 250 g fruit cake.
6 cups pure sieved icing sugar
½ cup liquid glucose
1 tablespoon glycerine
5 teaspoons gelatine
¼ cup water
flavouring of own choice, several drops
Sift sugar into bowl. Place gelatine and water in small bowl, stand in saucepan in a little water, about 4 cm, and dissolve over gentle heat. Using this way to dissolve gelatine, you do not boil the mixture or lose any liquid in dissolving. Remove from heat, stir in glucose and glycerine until dissolved. Remove bowl from water and stir liquid into sieved sugar. Knead well until icing becomes smooth and pliable. Add colouring if liked, also flavouring to taste, and is ready to use. This quantity will cover a 20 × 20 cm or 250 g cake.

Add a little extra icing sugar if too soft, but if it is not going to be used for a while, store in airtight container at room temperature, then knead in the extra sugar when ready to use on cake.

Honey Glaze for Ham

½ cup honey
¼ cup brown sugar
1 teaspoon each soya sauce and dry mustard
1 tablespoon brown vinegar
Combine all ingredients in a bowl and brush over ham. Before applying glaze, cut surface fat into diagonal pattern to form diamond shapes. Brush well all over with the glaze and put into moderately hot oven for 30 minutes or until golden brown. Can decorate ham with cloves and halved glace cherries.

MUFFINS, SCONES AND BREAD

Homemade Crumpets

500 g plain flour
2 teaspoons sugar
7 g package Tandaco active dry yeast
600 mL milk
¼ teaspoon bi-carb soda
2 teaspoons salt
1 tablespoon water (warm)

In large bowl thoroughly mix 2 cups flour, sugar and undissolved yeast. Heat milk to lukewarm, gradually add to dry ingredients and blend well. Add remainder of flour and beat 5 minutes, scraping bowl occasionally. Cover and stand for about one hour, until mixture doubles in size. Dissolve salt and bi-carb soda in warm water and stir into mixture. Cover and allow to prove for 1 hour more. Heat heavy based frying pan (185°C for electric frypan). Grease egg rings and base of pan with oil. Pour in enough batter to nearly fill ring and allow to cook until top has set, about 5 minutes. Remove ring, turn crumpet and cook for a few seconds. Turn again and allow to dry thoroughly on the underside. Cool on wire rack. Toast and serve with butter.

Note: Excess batter may be covered and refrigerated for use the next day. When ready to use again, add one tablespoon of warm water and stir batter down.

Muffins

2 cups plain flour
2½ teaspoons baking powder
¼ teaspoon salt
3 tablespoons sugar
75 g melted margarine
1 cup milk
1 egg

Sift dry ingredients three times, drop in unbeaten egg. Add milk, half a cup at a time. Stir, do not beat. When partly mixed, add melted margarine. Stir only until mixed. Bake in greased patty tins in hot oven 190°C, 10–12 minutes. Makes 24. Serve hot with a knob of butter in the top of each muffin.

Walnut Mix Muffins

1 tablespoon butter
½ cup brown sugar
2 level teaspoons cinnamon
¾ cup chopped walnuts

Make plain muffin batter by sifting flour, baking powder, salt and then add sugar. Melt together butter and golden syrup. Beat egg in basin, add milk, then stir in melted ingredients together with vanilla. Pour this liquid into the dry ingredients and stir into a batter. Stir for only 15 to 20 seconds, just until the flour is dampened. Mixture will be lumpy but do not attempt to stir out lumps. Add half the walnut mixture to the batter. Pour into muffin tins, filling two-thirds full. Sprinkle rest of walnut mixture over top of uncooked muffins. Bake in hot oven for 15 to 20 minutes.

Light Scones

2 level cups self-raising flour
¼ teaspoon salt
1 dessertspoon icing sugar
2 level dessertspoons butter or margarine
¾ cup milk

Sift flour, salt and icing sugar together. Lightly rub shortening into mixture. Mix thoroughly to a soft dough with milk. Knead on floured board, press out 18 mm thick and cut into shapes. Bake on a greased or floured tray in hot oven, 220°C for 12 to 15 minutes.

Fluffy Pikelets

1 cup self-raising flour
pinch salt
¼ teaspoon bi-carb soda
2 tablespoons sugar
1 egg
½ cup sour milk or fresh milk with
     1 teaspoon vinegar
1 dessertspoon melted butter

Sift dry ingredients. Add sugar, egg, milk. Beat until smooth and thoroughly mixed. Beat on high speed in blender for 1 minute, fold in melted butter. Place in spoonfuls on hot griddle or 150°C frypan. Turn to brown on both sides. Use a cut, raw potato for rubbing over the pan when cooking pikelets. This eliminates the use of melted butter for greasing.

Homemade Bread

1 kg flour
1 tablespoon sugar
2 teaspoons salt
7 g Tandaco active dry yeast
4 tablespoons full cream powdered milk
600 mL hot tap water
2 g butter
egg (optional)

Sift half of flour and all other dry ingredients into bowl. Heat liquid ingredients including butter or other fat and egg when used. Add water to dry ingredients and beat 2 minutes at medium speed of electric mixer or 300 strokes by hand, scraping bowl occasionally. Stir in enough additional flour to make a soft dough. Turn out on to lightly floured board, knead until smooth and elastic. Cover with overturned bowl. Let rise until double in bulk. Punch dough down. Divide dough into portions used in recipe and continue with shaping and panning instructions as in recipe. Cover with cloth and let rise in warm place free from draught until double in bulk or bread reaches top of tin.

Loaf bread bakes in 200°C oven for 35 to 40 minutes. Rolls, buns and cakes bake at 200°C for 15 to 20 minutes unless otherwise stated in recipe.

Punching down: Push your fist into the centre of dough. Pull the edges of the dough to the centre and turn the dough over. Makes 2 loaves.

Wholemeal Bread

1 kg wholemeal self-raising flour
1 teaspoon salt
7 g Tandaco active dry yeast
1 tablespoon sugar
600 mL warm water

Follow basic instructions (*see Homemade Bread recipe*). Divide dough in half and shape into loaves. Place in 2 greased loaf tins. Prove until dough nearly fills tin. Bake at 200°C for 35 to 40 minutes. Makes 1 loaf.

FETE FAVOURITES
Coconut Ice

4 cups sugar
1 cup evaporated milk
2 tablespoons glucose
1 cup desiccated coconut
cochineal

Combine sugar, milk and glucose in saucepan and heat on low until sugar dissolves. Bring to boil and heat on low 20–25 minutes or until a small amount forms a soft ball when dropped in water.

Remove from heat and stir in coconut. Press half mixture into greased square tin. Add 2 drops cochineal to remaining mixture and stir. Press pink mixture onto white and allow to set and cool.

Turn out and cut into squares.

Old Fashioned Fudge

3 cups sugar
pinch salt
½ cup cocoa
1 cup milk
2 tablespoons liquid glucose
45 g butter or substitute
1 teaspoon vanilla

The right degree of heat is essential for success in this economical, delicious fudge. To gauge correct heat, a sweets thermometer is necessary.

In saucepan combine sugar, salt, cocoa, milk and glucose, stir over low heat until sugar dissolves. Boil rapidly until mixture reaches 117°C. Add vanilla, beat until fudge loses its gloss and starts to change colour. Pour into greased and lined 20 cm square sandwich tin. Cut into squares when cold.

Toffee Apples

500 g sugar
¾ cup water
2 tablespoons brown vinegar
wooden skewers
red colouring

Insert skewers in apples. Boil sugar, water and vinegar together then allow to simmer until the syrup sets hard when a little is dropped into cold water. Stand saucepan in a basin of boiling water. Add colouring and stir. Should be a good bright red. Then dip apples into toffee, drain for a second, then stand on greased paper until hard.

Caramel Popcorn

½ cup golden syrup
¼ teaspoon salt
1 tablespoon butter
½ cup brown sugar
½ teaspoon vanilla
8 cups popped corn
Bring syrup, sugar and salt to boil. Cook slowly for 6 minutes. Then add vanilla and butter and pour over popcorn. Coat well.

Numbers Toffee

2 tablespoons butter
4 tablespoons vinegar
6 drops vanilla essence
8 tablespoons sugar
Put all ingredients in a saucepan and bring to boil. Boil until firm when put into cold water. It is most important that the mixture is not stirred. When cooked, pour into greased dish and mark into squares. When cold, cut into squares.

Peanut Brittle

150 ml water
2 cups sugar
1 teaspoon glucose liquid
½ teaspoon cream of tartar
1 dessertspoon butter
½ cup unsalted nuts
Place sugar and water in a medium sized saucepan, stir until dissolved, add cream of tartar and glucose, boil to 320°F. Should be a very pale brown shade. Remove from heat, add butter and nuts, mix well. Pour on to buttered slab tin. Break into pieces when cold. Note: any firm nuts like almonds, brazils, cashew or hazelnuts may be used in place of peanuts. A combination of nuts is very tasty. Care must always be taken to remove skins before using for toffee.

JAMS AND RELISHES
Peach and Passionfruit Jam

1   kg peaches
1 dozen passionfruit
lemon juice
900 g sugar
Peel peaches and cut into slices, cover with half the sugar and leave until the next day. Boil until tender, then add remainder of sugar, lemon juice and passionfruit with some of the seeds strained out. Boil 1½ hours or until the mixture sets when tested.

Fruit Salad Jam

4 large oranges
3 bananas
1 medium pineapple
2 kg sugar
1400 ml water

Wash oranges and slice thinly, cover with the water and stand overnight. Next day place in a large saucepan and boil steadily for 30 minutes, until rind is tender. Add finely chopped pineapple and warmed sugar. Boil approx. 1½ hours until jam jells when tested on a cold saucer. Remove from heat and stir in finely sliced bananas. Allow jam to stand 5 minutes before bottling into sterilised jars. Seal when cold. Makes almost 2 litres of jam.

Rhubarb and Ginger Jam

2 kg rhubarb
1 cup water
¼ cup lemon juice
5 cm piece fresh root ginger
1½ kg sugar
½ cup finely chopped crystallised ginger

Wash and trim rhubarb, cut into 2½ cm pieces. Put into saucepan, add water and lemon juice, bring to boil. Peel and slightly crush the fresh ginger, add and reduce heat, simmer until rhubarb is soft, then remove the ginger. Add sugar and cook over low heat, stirring constantly, until sugar is dissolved. Stir in crystallised ginger, bring to boil. Boil rapidly for about 10 minutes or until jam has reached setting point. Pour into warm sterilised jars and seal immediately.

Lemon Lime Marmalade

750 g lemons and limes
7½ cups water
6 cups sugar

Wash and dry fruit. Slice finely, putting seeds in a muslin bag. Put fruit in large saucepan with water and seeds. May be soaked overnight if you like. Cook gently until soft and half liquid has evaporated, about 1½ hours. Remove muslin bag, drain fruit well but do not force as this clouds the marmalade. Measure liquid. For each cup add 1 cup sugar. Stir until sugar has dissolved. Bring to boil and cook rapidly until setting point is reached in 15 to 20 minutes. Take pan off heat and skim the top. Stand for 15 minutes then ladle into warm jars. Cover and seal.

Apricot Passionfruit Jam

4 cups boiling water
juice 2 lemons
12 passionfruit
200 g dried apricots, halved
4 cups sugar

Cut passionfruit in halves, remove pulp and reserve. Place washed shells in saucepan, cover with water. Boil until soft, scoop out remaining pulp, discard thin shell. Chop pulp finely, add to seeds and juice.

Wash apricots thoroughly. Cover with boiling water, stand a few hours to soften. Place apricots and water in which they soaked into large saucepan, boil until soft and pulpy. Add passionfruit, sugar and lemon juice, stir over low heat until all sugar has dissolved, then bring to boil. Boil quickly until jam jells when tested. Fill into hot sterilised jars, seal and label when cold. Makes 1200 ml.

Sugarless Strawberry Jam

250 g strawberries hulled
4 artificial sweetener tablets
1 teaspoon powdered gelatine
1 tablespoon water
1 teaspoon lemon juice

Cooking time about 30 minutes. Quarter strawberries and place in a heavy pan over low heat until the juice runs. Boil quickly for 5 minutes. Add the artificial sweetener. Dissolve gelatine in the water and lemon juice over low heat. Add to fruit. Turn into a bowl and when cold, refrigerate. This jam will not keep for more than 1 week and must be stored in the fridge.

Note. Can be made equally well with raspberries, apricots, peaches, blackberries and other fruit. Try adding chopped blanched almonds to apricot and peach jam.

Tomato Jam

1.5 kg tomatoes
500 g apples
1 tablespoon grated lemon rind
⅓ cup lemon juice
grated rind of 1 lemon
1.25 kg sugar

Skin tomatoes and cut into thin slices. Put tomatoes, peeled and cored and thinly sliced apples and grated lemon rind into large saucepan. Cover, bring to boil, reduce heat, simmer 30 minutes. Put sugar into baking dish, place into moderate oven for 7 minutes. Add sugar and lemon juice to tomato mixture. Stir until sugar is dissolved. Bring to boil. Boil uncovered about 40–45 minutes or until jam jells when tested on cold saucer. Stir occasionally during cooking time. Pour into hot sterilised jars. Seal. Makes about 1.5 litres or 6 cups.

Uncooked Fruit Relish

2 large cooking apples, peeled
1 large white onion
1 red capsicum, halved and seeded
1 cup seedless raisins
2 tablespoons vinegar
1 level teaspoon salt
1 teaspoon sugar

Mince apples, onion, capsicum and raisins. Add remaining ingredients. Put into glass jars. Cover. May be served after 24 hours, with cold meat.

Corn Relish

3 level tablespoons cornflour
1 level tablespoon mustard
2 level teaspoons each turmeric and celery seed
1 level teaspoon curry powder
2½ cups white vinegar
1¾ cups white sugar
750 g freshly cooked corn stripped from cob or 2 × 420 g cans whole kernel corn drained
¼ cup each finely chopped red pepper and green pepper
1 large onion finely chopped

Blend cornflour, mustard, turmeric, curry powder, celery seed with ¼ cup of the vinegar. Place remaining vinegar and sugar in saucepan, bring to boil. Add corn, peppers and onion, cook gently for 20 minutes. Add blended ingredients and cook a further 5 minutes. Allow to cool, bottle and seal. Makes about three medium sized jars.

Apple Chutney

1.8 kg cooking apples peeled, cored and chopped
4 onions, peeled and finely chopped
2 cloves garlic, crushed
juice 1 lemon
1 tablespoon mustard seeds
900 ml vinegar
250 g raisins
1 tablespoon ground ginger
2 teaspoons salt
1 kg soft brown sugar

Place apples, onions, garlic, lemon juice, mustard seeds and 600 ml of the vinegar in preserving pan. Bring to boil, reduce heat and simmer for 1 hour until mixture is soft. Add raisins, ground ginger, salt, sugar and remaining vinegar. Simmer, stirring often until chutney is thick. Ladle into jars and seal.

Plum Chutney

500 g green apples
500 g onions
1 kg plums (weighed after stoning)
250 g raisins
250 g sultanas
1 tablespoon salt
1 teaspoon ground allspice
½ teaspoon cayenne pepper
½ teaspoon dry mustard
½ teaspoon nutmeg
¼ teaspoon ground cloves
1 cup brown sugar
4 cups malt vinegar

Peel, core and finely chop apples and peeled onions. Coarsely chop plums. Put all ingredients in saucepan, bring to boil, stirring until sugar dissolves. Simmer, stirring occasionally, for 1½ to 2 hours or until thick. Turn into warm sterilised jars and seal airtight.

Tamarillo Chutney

1 kg tamarillos
450 g onions
450 g cooking apples
12 whole allspice berries
3 slices root ginger
170 g seedless raisins
600 ml vinegar
1 tablespoon salt
½ teaspoon cayenne pepper
680 g brown sugar

Blanch and peel tamarillos, chop into small pieces. Peel and chop onions and apples. Tie allspice and ginger in a piece of muslin. Put all ingredients in a large saucepan and simmer 2 hours, stirring from time to time. Remove allspice and ginger. Pour into hot sterilised jars. Seal when cold. Makes about 1.8 kilos.

Beetroot Pickle

6 medium-size beetroot
1200 ml malt vinegar
16 g each whole black pepper and allspice
1 small horseradish, grated
salt to taste, add a little at a time

Wash beetroot well, taking care not to break skins, and bake in moderate oven 1½ hours. When cool enough to handle, remove skins, cut beetroot into even slices and place in jars. Meanwhile boil together vinegar, horseradish, pepper and spice, let mixture become quite cold, then pour over beetroot. Cover jars and store in cool place.

Cucumber Dill Pickles

12 small cucumbers
4 sprays dill
1 spray basil
1 sprig each tarragon and rosemary
1 sage leaf
1 bay leaf
1 dried chilli
4 cloves garlic
4 to 6 crushed black peppercorns
few caraway seeds
¾ cup salt

Place all ingredients except cucumbers in a large saucepan. Add cucumbers, cover with boiling water. Make sure water is boiling as this ensures crisp cucumbers. Put lid on saucepan and leave to cool. When cold, pour into large screw top jars making sure brine covers the cucumbers. Store for at least 2 weeks. Keep in jar in refrigerator after opening.

Capsicum Preserve

500 g red and green capsicums without
    seeds, cored and cut into quarters or
    eighths lengthwise
⅓ cup coarse salt
3 cups water
3 cups white vinegar
extra dessertspoon coarse salt
2 teaspoons whole black peppercorns

Place capsicum strips, salt and water in basin, stirring occasionally to dissolve salt. Leave 24 hours. Drain and rinse well. Pack capsicums into hot sterilised jars. Combine vinegar, extra salt and peppercorns in saucepan and simmer 5 minutes. Fill jars and seal while hot. Use after 3 days.

CORNED BEEF
Tasty Hint

■ When boiling corned beef add quarter cup vinegar and 4 tablespoons treacle to the water. Gives meat a good colour and makes it juicy.

■ Quick meal: Heat a can of corned beef, remove from tin and put in a baking dish. Mix juice of half an orange, ¼ cup brown sugar and ¼ teaspoon dry mustard. Spoon over meat, heat through in a moderate oven for about 10–15 minutes. Any leftover meat can be used instead of the canned corned beef.

Too Salty?

■ Should soup, vegetables, stock or gravy remind you of Lot's wife, add a small quantity of coarse brown sugar and stir well.

■ When cooking salted meat like corned beef, soak overnight or boil for about 15 minutes, then throw away water and put the meat in fresh water. Cook as usual. The first boil takes away most of the salt.

■ Add whole peeled potato (not pieces) and simmer with stock for 15 to 20 minutes. Will absorb surplus salt and then can be lifted out and discarded.

■ Remove pan from heat. Gradually stir in 150 ml thin cream, evaporated milk or yoghurt. Warm through without boiling. This is recommended for over-salted soups.

CREAM
Helpful Tips

■ When whipping cream for cakes, add a small pinch bicarbonate of soda. Keeps cream fresh for days.

■ Sweeten cream with honey. It will stay firmer and keep whipped longer.

■ Cream will whip more easily if you add a few drops of lemon juice or a little dissolved gelatine.

■ Make more whipped cream by folding in one stiffly beaten egg white to every 200 ml of cream.

Clotted Cream

■ Choose a wide, shallow earthenware pan. Strain very fresh milk into this and leave to stand, overnight if summertime or for 24 hours in cold weather. Slowly, and without simmering, raise the temperature of the milk over a low heat until a solid ring of cream starts to form around the edge. Without breaking the cream by shaking the pan, very carefully remove it from the heat and leave overnight, or a little longer, in a cool place. The thick crust of cream can then be skimmed off the surface with a large spoon or a fish slice and placed in a glass dish for the table. Do not use pasteurised milk.

■ Very creamy milk is placed in a shallow pan or bowls and left until cream rises to the top. The milk is then scalded for about 1 hour by placing the pan or bowls over a pan of water maintained at a temperature of about 82°C. The cream is ready when straw coloured and wrinkled in appearance. It is then cooled overnight for about 12 hours. When cool, cream should be skimmed off the surface using a perforated skimmer or a shallow spoon. If the skimmed cream is left in refrigerator for a few hours it will thicken further. Alternatively, clotted cream can be made using the direct scald method. Double cream is placed in shallow pans or bowls and scalded as for the traditional method. After scalding and cooling the whole contents of the pan are used as clotted cream.

Cream for Cakes

■ When whipping cream for fillings and decorating, add 1 level tablespoon vanilla Instant Pudding Mix to 300 ml chilled cream. When the cream is piped or used as filling, it holds its shape beautifully. The pudding mix sweetens and flavours the cream at the same time.

CROCHET
To Stiffen Crochet

■ Wet crochet. Dip in solution of 2 cups sugar boiled in 1 cup water. Stretch crochet into correct shape on flat surface. Stuff with paper to hold in shape if necessary. Upright parts can be held in place with a stick. Allow to dry completely, adjusting as necessary to ensure correct shape is held. Drying may take 36 to 48 hours.

■ Make either boiled starch or a solution of one dessertspoon of liquid glue to 2 dessertspoons hot water. Immerse crochet, then place on a clean flat surface to dry. If stiffening pieces like crochet swans, when nearly dry, pin into shape on hard cardboard covered with plastic. Shape swans' bodies by stuffing with tissue paper, pull neck up and bend into shape.

■ If crochet only needs slight stiffening, use a solution of 12 ml starch to half a litre of hot water and dab lightly over the article. Should be placed on piece of white paper or clean cardboard to prevent sticking when drying. If needed, press article lightly with hot iron.

■ Use 2 envelopes gelatine dissolved in boiling water, add tablespoon epsom salts, plus a dash of methylated spirit if sheen is required. Stir until dissolved then add sufficient cold water to completely immerse article. Leave soaking for a few minutes, then spread out on towel to dry.

CROUP

Make a solution of 3 parts vinegar, 2 parts methylated spirits, one part water. Soak a flannel strip in the solution and wrap around the child's neck.

CROÛTONS

Cut bread slices into 1 cm cubes. Fry in butter or oil. Drain well and sprinkle lightly with salt before serving. Croûtons fried in dripping are delicious with pea soup.

CRYSTALLISED FRUIT
Candied Peel

■ Make a brine by boiling 600 ml water and 110 g salt. Cut 6 lemons or oranges in half, pour brine over and soak for 3 days. Lift out, drain on wire drainer for 24 hours. Make syrup of 680 g sugar and 900 ml water and boil for 10 minutes. Remove pulp from fruit and place rind in boiling syrup. Cook fully for 20 minutes. Lift out and drain for 4 days on wire drainer. Reboil for 20 minutes again on the last day in the same syrup. Allow to cool in syrup then lift out, drain for 3 or 4 days and store in a dry place in airtight jars.

■ Crystallised Lemon Peel. Cut lemon peel in halves, quarters or thin strips, 2 cm long. Cover with salted water, 1 teaspoon to 600 ml of water, stand overnight. Drain and rinse in cold water. Cover with fresh clear water and simmer until tender, changing water two or three times to remove bitter flavour. When quite soft, drain and place in boiling syrup sufficient to cover peel. Use 2 cups of sugar and one cup water for sugar syrup. Cook until peel is clear. Drain syrup from peel and roll in sugar, spread to dry. When thoroughly dry, store in screw top jars.

Crystallised Ginger

■ The ginger must be perfectly ripe, firm and free from taint, young and non-stringy. Enamel or Corning Ware saucepans are best to use. Using a vegetable peeler, skin green ginger roots, then cut into suitably sized pieces or shapes. Cover with cold water for 1¼ hours, then drain. Cover with fresh water, if possible use rain water, and simmer at boil until the ginger can easily be pierced with straw.

■ For 1 kg green ginger, combine 2 cups sugar and 1 cup cold water, stir over low heat until sugar has dissolved, then add half level teaspoon cream of tartar. Bring to boil and simmer about 5 minutes until slightly thickened. Add ginger and slow boil 10 minutes. Stand 24 hours. Next day drain syrup from ginger, add 1 cup sugar and stir over low heat until dissolved, then bring to boil and pour over ginger. Stand another 24 hours. Repeat next day, adding further cup of sugar, stand for 2 days. Strain and spread on flat baking sheet. Dry very carefully in open oven at 120°C.

■ **Crystallised Preserved Ginger**: Dissolve 1 kg loaf sugar in 1½ cups cold water. Put on stove and bring slowly to boiling point, ensuring all grains are dissolved before reaching this point. Allow syrup to boil until 105°C is reached. Remove from heat and allow to stand undisturbed until it has cooled to 32°C. Stand ginger on a low wire mesh rack and place in a container. Pour over crystal syrup and allow to stand several hours until a thin crust of crystallised sugar forms on surface of syrup. Carefully raise wire rack from syrup and drain. Place fruit in very cool oven and dry until crystals are formed over fruit. Stand in a warm place until fruit is thoroughly dry.

■ Crystallised fruit should be packed in an airtight container, with waxed paper between each layer. Left-over syrup can be used as a dessert sauce, or for making toffee with addition of a little butter and 1 teaspoon of vinegar. It also may be bottled and sterilised for re-use.

Crystallised Cherries

Only firm and unbruised cherries are suitable. Stone the cherries, then prepare a syrup. Loaf or lump sugar is best as it contains fewer impurities. To avoid danger of sugar boiling over and catching fire, first grease preserving pan with good salad oil or butter. Use two parts sugar to one of water. Warm sugar in oven before gradually adding to boiling water. Boil to 100°C, the large thread stage. Put cherries into pan with sufficient boiling syrup to cover them. Boil up three or four times, skimming each time. Remove from heat, take out of syrup and drain on sieve. Place on wire trays and put in cool oven until crystallised then put in suitable storage jars or boxes.

CUCUMBERS

To keep fresh and crisp, place the stalk end in a jar of water.

CUPBOARDS

Freshen stale-smelling cupboards. Mix 2 tablespoons ammonia in water in an old cup or small bowl and leave to stand in cupboard overnight.

CURRY
Tasty Tips

■ When making curry, add a slice of fruit cake instead of the usual sultanas or raisins. This greatly improves the flavour.
■ Grate in a raw potato about 15 minutes before serving a curry. Easier and better than flour for thickening.

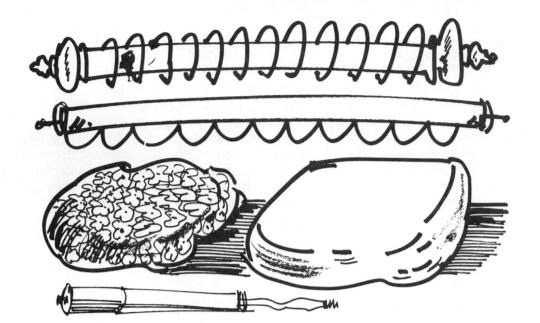

CURTAIN RODS

Wax curtain rods before replacing laundered curtains. The curtains will slide on easily and the wax will prevent the rods rusting.

CURTAINS

To restore whiteness to terylene curtains, soak them for 5 minutes in a mixture of 5 litres of water, ¼ cup Zixo bleach and 1 teaspoon vinegar. Then rinse well.

CUSHIONS

■ Do your old feather cushions need **refluffing**? Open a seam, insert the tube of a bicycle pump, and pump air into feathers.
■ Break a piece of camphor into small pieces and mix with the filling when making cushions. The camphor will ensure **fresh cushions** and keep the moths away.
■ Make a cushion like a tea-cosy to fit on the back of a baby's high chair. Will **save baby's head** from many a bang.

CUTLERY
Cleaning Pearl Handles on Knives

■ Cover handles with paste of lemon juice and French chalk. Leave 2 or 3 hours, then remove with hot water. Or use a paste of peroxide and cream of tartar. Or dip a cloth in eau-de-cologne, then in fine powdered whiting. Rub handles, polish with soft clean cloth. This is also good for piano keys.
■ Use 2 tablets of Steradent (for false teeth) to 1200 ml of warm water. Soak handles for three hours, rinse and dry.

Bright Silver Plate

■ Add a few drops of ammonia to the washing water to keep silver plate bright.

Discoloured Ivory

■ Moisten whiting with lemon juice and apply with soft old toothbrush, leave a few minutes, rinse in water to which a little borax has been added. Or make a stiff paste of whiting and 6% peroxide. Apply like a poultice, put in sun and leave until paste sets or dries. Wash off and dry.

■ Rub with a cloth dampened either in methylated spirits or eau-de-cologne.

■ Mix equal parts of powdered whiting, methylated spirits and eau-de-cologne, apply to handles and leave overnight. Remove and clean in usual way.

■ Ivory handles on knives and forks can be restored by rubbing with the cut surface of half a lemon lightly dipped in salt.

■ A cake of camphor stored in your box of good cutlery will stop tarnishing and keep away any musty smell.

CUTLETS

■ Add grated cheese to the breadcrumbs for cutlets. Makes a tasty change.

■ Add one dessertspoon of oil to the beaten egg when crumbing fish or cutlets. Makes crumbs stick firmly.

■ After coating in flour, dip cutlets or fish in half a cup hot water, containing 1 level teaspoon gelatine. Lastly dip in crumbs.

D

DATES

Add lemon juice to dates before putting them through a mincer. They will run through without sticking.

DENTAL PLATES

To keep dental plates white, use toothpaste with dry bicarbonate of soda. All stains will disappear and the plate will be clean and sweet.

DESSERTS

■ See recipes under *Cooking*.

DIETING
Hints for a Svelte You

■ Eat breakfast. If you don't, fatigue and hunger will upset you.

■ Do not have any liquids with meals. Slowly sip them immediately after eating or between times.

■ Drink 600 ml of skim milk and six glasses of water each day.

■ For high kilojoule foods, substitute low kilojoule, sugar-free stewed fruits, skim milk, protein or low-starch breads.

■ Be sparing with salt at table and in cooking.

■ Avoid fried and breaded foods.

■ Include one hot dish in every meal or follow meals with hot beverage.

■ Count the kilojoules in the foods you taste while cooking.

■ Vary menus and serve food in dainty, tempting ways.

■ Regulate meal hours, so you eat at the same time each day.

■ Weigh once each week before breakfast. Weighing more frequently gives an inaccurate and often discouraging picture of progress.

■ Take time out for a 15-minute walk on good days.

■ Don't laze about. Find a new interest and get stuck into it.

■ Talk about anything but diet. The subject unsettles your will-power and bores your friends.

How to Think Thin

■ Put away your scales. They are a constant reminder that you are overweight and create stress, anxiety and fear of failure. Let your clothes be your guide.

■ When you look in the mirror, don't be disgusted. Imagine yourself getting thinner and like yourself as you are. The more you accept yourself the way you are, the easier it will be for the thin you to emerge.

■ Begin each day with some deep breaths and feel yourself relaxing. Close your eyes for a few moments and visualise the slim person you would like to be. Feel what it will be like to be thin. This will put you in the right frame of mind for a thin and relaxed day.

■ Forget past dieting failures. Concentrate on your success, even though you are still overweight. Keep the image of the trim, slim you in mind all the time. This is the start of natural appetite control.

■ When you sit down to eat, don't be afraid of food. You control food. It doesn't control you. The more you think of yourself as a thin person, the more you will eat like one.

■ Be daring when you shop for clothes. Begin to see yourself wearing new slim fashions. Imagine yourself in them, even if you can't wear them yet. This will help to fashion your new self-image. Soon you will be wearing the clothes you always wanted.

■ Don't get caught in competition games, comparing yourself with others who are also trying to lose weight. You will increase pressure on yourself. Move at your own individual pace. Just be conscious of yourself and your goals.

■ If you overeat occasionally, don't feel guilty. Guilt can propel you into a binge.

■ Become aware of what you think of yourself. If you think of yourself in a negative way, change your thoughts to positive ones. As your self-image improves, so will your body.

DOGS

■ Prevent puppies from **chewing** on things by sprinkling red pepper or oil of cloves on the objects.

■ Put mothballs in the garden to discourage **stray dogs**. They last for several weeks.

■ See also *Cat and Dog Repellants*.

DOLLS

Hold dented doll parts over a steaming kettle or saucepan of boiling water for one minute. If not successful, repeat and dents should pop out. Also works for ping pong balls.

DRAINS

To clear choked drains, put a large handful of washing soda crystals over the sink outlet and pour down a kettle of boiling water.

DRAWERS

■ Rub a little floor polish on the sides of stubborn drawers which stick, and polish well.

■ Drawers will run smoothly if you smooth runners with fine sandpaper, then rub runners and bearers with dry soap or candle wax.

■ Tack a strip of wide elastic inside the front of your dressing table drawer to hold cosmetic jars and bottles.

DRIED FLOWERS

After arranging dried flowers, lightly dust with hair spray, to make flowers long-lasting.

DRIED FRUIT

■ Tip fruit into a colander and spread with the hands. Then stand colander on saucepan of boiling water for a few minutes. The steam makes the fruit **soft and moist**.

■ Empty mixed fruit into a screw topped jar and pour in a little sweet wine, sherry, marsala or similar, sufficient to moisten the fruit. Shake well and let stand for a while. As well as **softening the fruit**, this gives a nice flavour.

■ **Dried prunes** will keep 12 months or longer in packets or jars. If they get too much air, a white mould grows on the fruit. So keep them in airtight containers.

How to Dry Stone Fruits

■ Use only fresh, ripe fruit. Wipe and lay on oven trays or other suitable rack. Slice tins are very good. Dry in oven at temperature between 250°C to 300°C. Heat should be raised slowly to prevent hard skins which prolong the process of evaporation from the centre of fruit.

■ When fruit has been removed from the oven, allow to cool for 12 hours at room temperature. Pack in wooden or cardboard boxes lined with greaseproof paper and store in a very dry place.

DRIFTWOOD

Driftwood looks twice as effective if it is bleached. Treat the wood with alternate applications of ammonia and hydrogen peroxide until the required shade is obtained. Treated this way, driftwood looks beautiful with floral or greenery arrangements.

DRIPPING

To keep dripping clean, pour a tablespoon of boiling water into the basin of hot fat. The impurities will collect in the water at the bottom of the basin.

DUSTERS

Soak dusters in turpentine and allow to dry. They collect the dust much better.

DYEING
Dyeing Pampas Grass

■ It is important to pick pampas when the fluffy head is just starting to burst out of the calyx. This means it is still in the state when it will take up water and any dye colouring in the water. Do not use dry pampas as it will just disintegrate. Make a dye of crêpe paper, using any colour needed, by pouring boiling water on the crêpe paper in a deep pot. Stand stems of pampas grass to absorb the dye mixture for about 24 to 48 hours. The grass can also be completely dipped into a bucket of the dye mixture until colour takes on but this is a lot messier.

■ Using the same procedure, vegetable dyes in water give a solution quite deep in colour.

To Dye a Lampshade

Make the linen fabric on the shade evenly wet all over using warm water and a brush or sponge. Then a hot solution of Rit Dye and water can be brushed on, using even strokes in the colour of your choice.

EARWIGS
Banish Earwigs

■ Take medium-size flower pots of any shape or material. Plug the bottom holes and loosely pack down with moist hay or dried grass from your garden.

Place upside down where earwigs congregate. Put a one cent coin under the edge of each pot to provide the earwigs with virtually invisible access. This is the ideal dark, warm and cosy home they look for, and they will gather there in hundreds. Once a week or fortnight, pick the pot up and shake the contents into the fire. Hay and earwigs go up in smoke!

■ Mix equal quantities of borax and sugar with water to form a thin paste. Place in saucers or lids near the infested areas. A sure cure!

EGG CARTONS

Use an empty egg carton to store reels of thread in a drawer. This uses little storage space and keeps reels neatly together.

EGGS
Twenty-One Hints for Eggs

■ Beat egg whites to an **easy froth** by heating the beaters for a few minutes before using.

■ One egg will go as far as two for **scrambling**, if you add a tablespoon fine breadcrumbs and one tablespoon milk to each egg.

■ A dessertspoon of vinegar in the pan when poaching eggs, **prevents yolks breaking** and keeps whites snowy.

■ A pinch of salt or three drops glycerine added to whites of eggs when beating will make the **froth stiffer**.

■ A little vinegar or a pinch of cream of tartar will increase the volume of **egg white** on whipping.

■ To **separate eggs**, break on to a saucer then cover the yolk with a small glass. Hold the yolk firmly on to the saucer and pour the white easily into another container.

■ **Left-over yolks** keep well without drying out for several days if placed in a glass and covered with melted butter (not too hot). Store in refrigerator.

■ When **boiling eggs** in an aluminium saucepan, put a teaspoon of salt in the water to prevent dark staining.

■ Good **egg flip** for invalids. Put one well-beaten egg into a tumbler with half teaspoon sugar and pinch salt. Fill up with hot milk and serve.

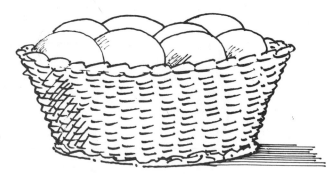

■ Use leftover chicken soup in **scrambled eggs** instead of milk.

■ When beating **egg yolks**, first rinse bowl with cold water. Beaten yolks slide out without sticking wastefully to sides.

■ **Scrambled eggs** are fluffier if you add 1 tablespoon evaporated milk for every 2 eggs.

■ Scrambled eggs will not become watery after cooking if you add cornflour to the milk. Use ½ level teaspoon cornflour to 3 eggs and ½ cup milk.

■ For delicious breakfast eggs, thicken some tomato juice, add a little salt and pepper and use in place of water when **poaching**. Serve eggs on toast with some of the sauce poured over them.

■ **Poach eggs** perfectly by putting them in boiling water for two seconds before breaking the shells. Also add a teaspoon of vinegar to the water in which they are cooked.

■ When **boiling eggs**, add a dessertspoon salt for each dozen. Once cooked, put saucepan with the eggs under running cold water. This direct action of the cold water on the hot eggs will make the shells very easy to peel. Try to keep eggs under the water as you peel.

■ Boil **cracked eggs** perfectly! Wrap tightly in a piece of foil, making a large twist at top of egg so it can be easily lifted from boiling water when cooked.

■ One tablespoon of gelatine added to a cake, will do as a **substitute** for three eggs. Dissolve gelatine in a little cold water for a few minutes, add enough boiling water to make a cupful. Whip mixture with egg beater until light, then add to other ingredients.

■ When using **hard-boiled eggs**, place in cold water as soon as cooked, then leave there. If yolks must be removed, put whites back in the cold water so they will not change colour.

■ Chop or mash **hard-boiled eggs** for sandwiches while still hot. Add a little butter and seasoning. This makes an easy spreadable paste.

■ To poach eggs successfully try using aluminium foil. Cut 10 cm squares of double thickness foil and form them into hollow cup shapes. Put a nut of **butter** or margarine in each and float in 25 mm of gently boiling water in a large pan. When the butter melts, break an egg into each cup, cover, and simmer for 4 to 6 minutes, or until the whites are firm. Lift cups carefully from pan, slide the eggs out and serve at once.

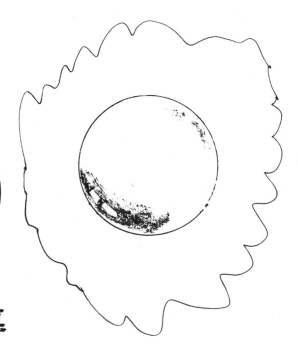

ELECTRIC MIXERS

Shortening will not stick to electric mixer beaters if they are heated in boiling water before use.

ENAMELWARE

Enamelware which is stained can be cleaned with salt moistened with turpentine.

EYES

Optometric experts say watching TV can strain your eyes if you sit too close or if the room is poorly lit. In a normally lighted room, people should sit at least five times the width of the screen away from the TV set. Another way to give the eyes some relief is to look frequently around the room or out the window.

FABRIC
To Take Dressing out of Fabrics

Soak fabrics overnight in a trough of cold water with 60 g epsom salts. Next day rinse well, then wash as usual in hot sudsy water.

Revive Dingy Whites

When white fabrics get dingy, yellow or grey, rinse and soak in cold water. Then make a solution of 9–11 litres of hot water, ½ cup liquid chlorine bleach and ½ cup detergent. Soak three or four hours in cool solution then wash as usual.

Goodbye Mildew

Remove mildew from cotton materials with household bleach. On wool and silk use 10 vol. strength peroxide from chemist, rinse off. Also good for mildew is a paste of ammonia and whiting.

FABRIC STIFFENER

■ For stiffening articles which cannot be starched such as taffeta petticoats, or as a substitute for commercial fabric stiffener for French flower-making, to stiffen linen, cotton and pure silk and lace, use **gelatine**.

Dissolve 3 teaspoons in 1 cupful hot water and stir until mixture is clear. Add 4 litres cold water. Use this as a final rinsing water to impart stiffness.

If article is too stiff when it is dry, simply rinse lightly with cold water and dry again. If it is not stiff enough, re-dip when it is dry. After the article is dry, damp it down, roll it dampen evenly, then iron. Petticoats which are sometimes required to be very stiff should be dipped twice, even 3 times. Use less gelatine to stiffen lace. One teaspoonful softened in 1 tablespoon hot water, added to 1 cup boiling water, will be sufficient.

■ To stiffen **hand crochet** with **sugar**, add 1 cup hot water to 1 cup sugar. Stir constantly over low heat until the sugar dissolves, then bring to simmering point. Cool slightly. Dip in the dry, thoroughly clean article. Pull it into shape and let dry. Re-dip two, even three times, until article is as stiff as required.

FACE MASKS
Egg Beauty Masks

Beat an egg yolk with 2 teaspoons lemon juice and 1 teaspoon honey until thick. Place on face and neck, leave until dry, about 10 minutes. Rinse off with cool water.

FEET

Keep feet cool and dry this summer with this lotion. Dissolve epsom salts in surgical spirit, pat into feet, allow to dry. Dust with talc. Also dust inside your shoes with talc or anti-perspirant powder.

Stop Burning Feet

■ Buy Shoe Stretch from shoe repairer. Pull out plastic inner soles from shoes; keep them as a pattern. Spray where inner soles were, then while wet, put on shoes and walk outside for a while. Ask shoe repairer to cut leather inner soles using the plastic ones as a pattern.

■ Dampen inner soles with methylated spirits, sprinkle into shoes and wear them. Will not stain the leather.

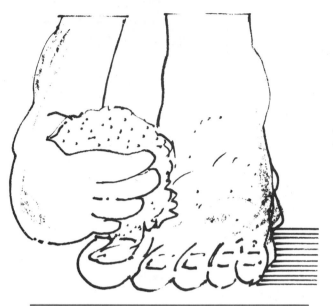

Tips for Feet

■ Do not stand, walk! Standing in one place causes the blood to stagnate in a long column in the arteries of the leg. Walking will assist the pumping action of the muscles to increase circulation and prevent ugly varicose veins and skin blemishes.

■ Do not sit with your legs or feet crossed, or your leg hooked around the chair. These positions can shorten the calf muscles or cause puffy ankles. Sit with your feet placed squarely in front of you, spaced a few inches apart.

■ Do not use pumice, razors or corn pads on your feet. These abrade and burn the skin around a corn or callus and only make them larger and uglier.

■ Do not walk barefoot unless on sand, turf, a thick rug or any other soft, yielding surface. Then it is the greatest foot exercise in the world. But walking barefoot on hard surfaces may bring on bruises.

■ See your podiatrist regularly. He or she is the best friend your feet have.

FERNS

A light sprinkling of epsom salts around roots of ferns after watering, especially maidenhair, makes them grow beautifully.

FINGERPAINT

Mix 1 heaped tablespoon cornflour with a little water until you get a thick, milky paste. Pour on some boiling water, stirring very quickly. Repeat very quickly until the paste turns thick, clear and smooth. If paste does not thicken, you may need to cook it for a little while. Add a little paint, dye or food colouring. Food colouring is best for the colour range as many different colours can be purchased from health food stores. Allow to cool before child uses the paint.

FIREPLACES
For a Clean Fireplace

■ Vinegar removes dirty marks from porous brick fireplaces. Use neat, dabbing on with piece of rag. Also brings out natural colour of bricks.

■ Smear sugar soap, obtainable at most paint stores, over smoke stained parts and leave overnight before sponging off with warm to hot soapy water, then rinse clean. Touch up the treated parts with a cement surface sealer, also from paint stores. Then proceed as normal to paint, or just leave as above.

■ To clean a hearth coated with Estapol and slightly burnt by ashes, scrub with medium grade glass paper. If the hearth is deeply burnt, it is not possible to treat at all, so remove Estapol with paint stripper first or with similar fluid.

FISH
Best Batters

■ **Crisp Fish Batter:**
Roll fish in self-raising flour, dip into a well-beaten egg and roll again in the flour.

■ **Batter for Fish or Fritters:**
Mix flour with 1 part vinegar to 3 parts water and add ½ teaspoon baking soda. This batter browns more quickly and is never greasy.

■ **Beer Batter:**
According to amount needed, mix one-third custard powder and two-thirds wholemeal self-raising flour. Pour sufficient flat beer into the mix, stirring continuously until a thick consistency is achieved.

Tips for Tasty Fish

■ For better **fried fish**, add 1 teaspoon vinegar to the batter and use water to mix batter instead of milk.

■ When **crumbing fish** or cutlets, after coating in flour, dip in half a cup hot water which contains 1 level teaspoon gelatine. Lastly dip in crumbs.

■ Add one dessertspoon of oil to the beaten egg when **crumbing fish** or cutlets. Makes crumbs stick firmly.

■ **Boiled fish** will stay intact if you follow these two rules. Do not cook in too much water or for too long.

■ See recipes under *Cooking*.

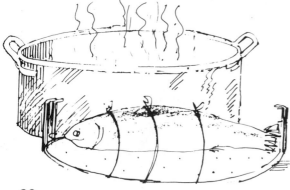

■ When **frying fish**, sprinkle a little curry powder in the pan first. This stops the smell and improves the flavour.

■ If **fish breaks up** in pan while cooking, try salting the fish and leaving for a few hours before using.

■ Rub fish to be scaled with vinegar first. **Scales** then come off easily.

■ Drain **fried fish** on stale pieces of bread instead of kitchen paper. The bread absorbs all fat.

FLEAS

Mineral turps sprayed from an atomiser on to the back of mats after cleaning will keep away fleas and silverfish.

FLIES
Keeping Flies at Bay

■ Clean windows with a cloth soaked in kerosene. Leave for 10 minutes to dry, then polish with dry cloth.

■ Keep flies away from kitchens by placing a piece of sponge rubber on an old saucer. Moisten with a teaspoon of oil of lavender and 2 tablespoons boiling water. Add a little hot water each day and the oil twice a week.

■ Sprinkle oil of lavender on a clean cloth and rub over window and door frames, window sills, and other places where flies come in and settle.

■ Rub a little paraffin oil on window glass and frames.

■ Tie a few cloves in a small piece of muslin and hang it on the light fitting. A pot of mint, tansy or flowers of the pyrethrum family plant on or near the window sill also deters flies.

■ A pot of fennel growing in kitchen or patio will keep flies away.

■ To make old-fashioned fly papers, cut strong paper into strips, then soak in a strong solution of alum. Dry before applying the following. Boil linseed oil and resin, remove from heat. Have ready some

Fly
Paper

melted honey and mix with oil and resin.
Apply to dried, alum-soaked paper.

■ Use herbs to repel flies around back
door. Then congratulate yourself on a
cheaper and healthier solution than spray
cans. Growing herbs where the leaves can
be pinched or trodden on to release the
aroma makes them more effective. Basil,
tansy and rue can be planted in clumps
near doorways. Mint is one of the best
repellants as it is also good for ants, aphids,
cabbage butterfly, caterpillars, fleas, beetles
and moths.

■ Pennyroyal is also good to repel flies,
fleas and mosquitoes. Wormwood is
another good herb to use as it makes a very
attractive shrub. Wormwood and rue
cannot be used in cooking as they have a
very bitter flavour.

■ Also try rubbing some onion juice on
the back door. Walnut trees, if you have the
space, repel stable flies and are good if you
have an animal being bitten by them
frequently.

FLOOR POLISH

■ Mix together 250 ml each kerosene and
vinegar. Shake well. Also good for cleaning
furniture, marble, paintwork, tiles. Note:
any stubborn marks on **lino** can be
removed by first rubbing with kerosene
and steel wool.

■ Grate 30 g of **beeswax** into a jar and
pour on a teacup of turpentine. Stand jar in
hot water until wax dissolves.

■ To remove **wax build-up** on floors, mix
4 tablespoons detergent and 150 ml
ammonia with a gallon warm water. Swab
floor sparingly with this, swirling it in with
a soft brush and leave for a few minutes.
Mop up, rinsing with clean cool water and
dry. When the floor is quite dry again,
apply new coating of wax and polish.

■ **Scratched varnished floors** can be
restored by rubbing over with a little lard,
then polishing with a clean cloth.

■ To remove smears from **polished floors**,
hand wash floor with warm (not hot) water
and a minimum of detergent. Wipe floors
along the same lines as the grain to prevent
smearing. Wipe off with a clean wet cloth
followed by a dry cloth. To maintain a good
surface, spray a film of kerosene from a fly
spray on to a polishing mop. Follow the
grain to eliminate smearing.

■ Stains on **terrazzo floors** can be
removed by rubbing the area with a slice of
lemon dipped in salt. Leave for an hour
before washing.

■ To restore shine to **floorboards**, firstly
clean thoroughly by scrubbing with warm
water and detergent. Allow to dry
thoroughly, then give a coat of clear Estapol
if high shine is desired. Give second coat
after 24 hours.

■ Apply **floor polish** with newspaper
instead of a cloth. Less polish is used as it
does not soak into the paper. Newspaper is
also good for polishing off as it gives a
lasting shine.

FLOWERS
For Cut Flowers That Last

■ Flowers with woody or semi-woody stems should have ends crushed or split before putting in vases so water intake is greater.

■ Adding an aspirin to the water may prolong your flowers' lives.

■ Freshly cut flowers last longer if the stems are wrapped in a 75 mm strip of foil.

■ Add one tablespoon of sugar to 1200 ml of water in vases for asters, chrysanthemums, daisies, petunias and sweet peas.

■ Hydrangeas will keep fresh for a week indoors if you split the stems one centimetre at base and stand in boiling water.

■ To keep cut flowers fresh longer, add a dessertspoon powdered alum to water for hydrangeas. For carnations, a teaspoon of sugar added to the vase keeps the flowers fresher and encourages buds to open. For all flowers, pick in the evening, never in the heat of the day.

■ To keep picked hibiscus flowers open at night, take a small amount of tobacco from a cigarette. Place in a saucer with a little tepid water. Let stand 10 minutes, then dab the water around the outer edge of each petal, all the way round. Cover and place in lower part of fridge for a while.

Keep Flowers on the Vine

To prevent flowers falling from vines, water well around roots, then sprinkle 500 g epsom salts around the roots and water in.

FORMICA

To restore badly faded, brown formica cupboards, try a good wipe-over with warm soapy water. Dry off immediately. Then apply a little linseed oil on a clean soft cloth, rub on to cupboards and give a final polish with Windex for a great shine.

FRAMES

See *Gilt Frames*.

FRENCH POLISH
Do It Yourself French Polish

Dissolve fresh orange shellac flakes in methylated spirits to make a reasonably thin solution. The timber surface should be free of dirt, finger marks and any abrasive streaks. Clean with turpentine or thinners, dust with a clean paint brush, then finally wipe with a clean lint-free rag. Apply the first coat with a lint-free brush using quick even strokes along the grain. Let dry about one hour then lightly sand using 6/0 paper. Apply second and successive coats until film is thick enough to show a slight sheen. There will be no penetration of these coats so the drying time will need to be longer before sanding. Do not sand after this stage.

Put several drops of boiled linseed oil into the mixture and apply with a cloth using a circular motion. As more and more coats are applied, add more drops of oil. Finally, to clean brushes used with shellac, use a mild solution of household ammonia and water followed by detergent and water.

French Polish Pick Me Up

To make a polish reviver, mix together ½ cup raw linseed oil, ¼ cup turpentine, 1 cup methylated spirits, 1 small bottle vinegar. Shake well, wash surface with mixture, let dry about 1 minute. Wipe dry, then polish with a second clean soft cloth.

FRUIT
To Ripen Fruit

■ Good way to ripen bananas is in a large plastic bag with either an apple, pear or quince. The gas given off by these fruits is a natural form of the synthetic gas used in the ripening sheds in packing houses.
■ Wrap green passionfruit in paper and put in a warm area. They'll ripen in no time.

FRUIT FLY
Traps

■ Using old bottles and tins, put into each a mixture of 1 teaspoon honey to 5 drops vanilla, well mixed. Hang these into trees after blossoms have finished flowering, as this mixture also attracts bees.
■ Mince two average size oranges, 20 g carbonate of ammonia, 90 ml water. Store mixture in screw top jar in fridge. To set lure, put 2 dessertspoons of mixture into plastic ice cream containers or bottles and add 300 ml water. Hang container in tree. Top water up every now and then to combat evaporation. Put a few holes around container to let flies in.

FRYPAN
Have it Gleaming Again

■ Remove dark grease marks from under an electric frypan, take off the frypan legs by undoing the screws. Saturate an old towel in household ammonia and lay it directly on the bottom of the pan. Put the towel and the pan in a large plastic bag, fastening it close to the handle with the control dial protruding from the bag. Leave overnight. Next day, remove the black corrosion with a scouring pad. This will make the pan like new. If corrosion is very bad, two applications might be necessary.

■ Dip steel wool in methylated spirits and rub stains lightly. Bicarbonate of soda on a cloth will give a final shine.

■ Remove thick, black marks with Sunbeam frypan cleaner which the makers put out themselves.

FUR
Coddle that Stored Mink

■ To store fur, make a cover of unbleached calico, sew up three sides and leave bottom end undone. Place over garment. Tie a piece of camphor to the hanger under the cover.

■ Sprinkle with epsom salts, wrap in tissue paper and put in plastic bag, with additional epsom salts inside and tie up the end. When items are needed again, just shake salts off and the furs are ready to wear. No smell to worry about. Epsom salts are good for storing almost anything.

■ Use zippered plastic blanket bags to ensure a perfect seal. Inside bag, put an unopened full tin of whole cloves. Pierce sides of tin with a vegetable knife to allow the smell of cloves to penetrate the bag. This saves a mess from loose cloves in bag. Each year renew the tin of cloves. Moths will never come near the smell of cloves. Also put a tin or two in wardrobes and cupboards where clothes are stored.

Spruce Up White Fur Fabric

Buy 500 g magnesia powder from the chemist, put an old towel or large pillow slip on the table, lightly rub powder on and through fur, fold with the fur facing outside, wrap in towel or put in pillow slip. Leave for a week then shake out and brush lightly using a soft brush. Can also be used to clean fur toys.

Fur Toys

Clean **furry toys** with a commercial carpet cleaner. Spray on, let dry, brush off or remove with nozzle of vacuum cleaner. For **plush and mohair toys**, clean by rubbing lightly with white spirit. Use in open air outdoors. The nap of the fur may be restored when dry by a light brushing with a suede shoe brush.

FURNITURE
Handy Hints

■ **White spots** on furniture will disappear if you mix together salt and olive oil and rub on. Leave for a while. This makes a good polish for all furniture except the highly polished kind.

■ Make your own **furniture reviver**. Mix half a litre of linseed oil with quarter litre each turpentine and vinegar, add one-eighth of a litre methylated spirits. Shake well before using.

■ For a **subtle scent** on your furniture, add a few drops of oil of cloves, attar of roses or oil of pine or lavender to your furniture cream or polish. Use in bedrooms, guest rooms, in the hall or for a quick polish up before entertaining.

■ **Heat marks** can be removed from polished wood by rubbing with a damp blue-bag until dark blue, then drying well with cloth and polishing in the usual way. Or mix cigarette ash with olive oil and work into the marks. Use tips of fingers and continue until marks disappear. Finish with soft cloth.

■ One or two drops of methylated spirits on a piece of cotton wool can also help remove heat marks. Rub the mark and a small area around it until the mark is not so noticeable. Then polish well in usual way.

Thin some raw linseed oil with turpentine and rub over the heat mark with a soft cloth, using only a few drops at a time. Keep rubbing until the mark goes or is less noticeable. Polish well.

■ **Rust** on chrome furniture can be removed by rubbing the area with crumpled aluminium foil.

■ For **surface scratches** on polished wood, rub lightly with a cork dipped in camphorated oil. When oil has worked in, polish.

■ To remove **white rings** on furniture made by wet glasses, mix equal quantities of linseed oil and turpentine. Rub on the white ring marks. Will remove easily. Apply your favourite polish afterwards.

■ To remove **heat marks** from furniture, apply a little furniture polish to the area, wiping off excess. Put three or four drops of ammonia on a damp cloth and rub heat marks carefully. Follow up immediately with more polish and rub up.

■ A small paint brush is ideal for cleaning **carved wood** furniture. Pour a little liquid polish in saucer and dip brush in from time to time as you brush.

■ Mix 280 ml each kerosene and vinegar. This makes a **cleaner and polisher** for furniture, tiles, marble, linoleum, paintwork.

■ Remove **water stains** from furniture by rubbing with a soft cloth dipped in camphorated oil.

■ To remove **sticky tape** from a varnished wood wardrobe, spray liberally with Windex spray-on window cleaner, leave for a while. Tape will come off leaving no tell-tale marks. Polish as usual.

■ Here's an easy way to remove **scratches** from furniture, especially darker furniture. Mix two parts olive oil to one part vinegar. Rub on with soft cloth.

■ To remove **perfume stains** from a polished table, treat stain with powdered pumice mixed to a thin paste with raw or boiled linseed oil. Rub lightly in direction of grain. Wipe with cloth dampened with plain linseed oil. Repeat as many times as necessary, then polish.

■ Using the finest sandpaper, very lightly go over the white perfume stain and wipe clean. Then very sparingly apply a well-blended fifty-fifty mixture of olive oil and vinegar with a piece of cotton wool, or very soft rag. After mixture dries on marks, apply another very sparing coat and let dry before polishing with a piece of flannelette or similar. Note: if furniture is a light colour, use white vinegar; if darker grained, try darker vinegar.

■ When **candle wax** falls on furniture, first chill it with an ice cube to make the wax easier to remove. Then prise off with a dull knife blade and polish wood in usual way.

■ **Lacquer** can be cleaned with sour milk and olive oil. Buff off with soft cloth.

■ To remove **scorch marks** caused by hot dishes on lacquered surface try Brasso, if ring marks are not too deep. Apply on piece of cotton material like an old singlet. Be sure you shake Brasso well and rub hard in a circular movement. The powder in Brasso has a cutting paste in it and will eventually cut rings out if they are not too deep. It might be easier to get Repo, the one with white powder included. As this is a lacquer reviver, you can apply all over the table. Do not just apply and wipe off; you really need elbow grease. After applying, use a piece of flannette to take the greasy look off table. Repo is found at car accessory departments.

■ If you polish **painted furniture** with a clear wax or cream, it is much easier to clean and does not require washing. Make your own polish by mixing a cup each of paraffin and vinegar and ½ cup linseed oil. Shake in a bottle and apply with a piece of flannelette. This is good for all painted woodwork.

■ Here's how to deal with **cigarette burns** on wooden furniture. Mix a paste of powdered pumice and linseed oil. Rub well in direction of grain. Remove with a cloth dipped in plain linseed oil and repolish.

■ To remove stains from **pigskin chairs**, rub with full strength Solyptol.

■ If **leather chairs** are dull, brighten by rubbing with half a lemon or stale beer. Polish with dry cloth.

■ To remove grease spots from a leather chair, rub well in a circular motion with eucalyptus oil. Then polish well.

■ If **glass scratches** are not too deep, rub over lightly with Goddards Silver Foam which contains jewellers rouge, a mild abrasive. If this doesn't work, try jewellers rouge rubbed on lightly and then polished off. Jewellers rouge is very hard to get, but is available at large hardware stores.

■ Some brands of toothpaste are quite successful for removing scratch marks on glass. Mix a level teaspoon of Silvo or Brasso with level teaspoon of white toothpaste, apply with a soft clean pad using a backwards and forwards movement. Cuts and polishes the scratches out. This is also good for scratches on perspex.

■ **Mildew** on furniture can be removed by rubbing over with a solution of one tablespoon of vinegar in a pint of warm water. Wipe off, dry and polish as usual.

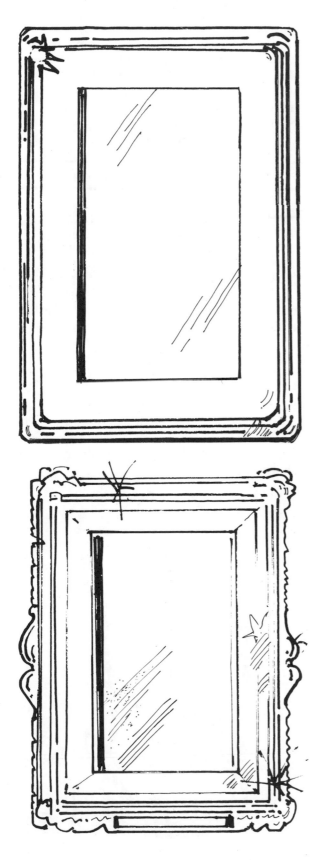

GALVANISED STEEL

To treat salt-corroded galvanised steel before painting, use phosphoric acid. Paint on, then cover with any zinc-rich paint.

GILT FRAMES
Removing Discoloration

■ Rub over with a clean cloth dipped in warm turpentine. Do not heat turpentine on the stove as it is highly inflammable, just stand the turpentine in a bowl of hot water.
■ Wipe over with equal parts of methylated spirits and water. Dry well.
■ Rub with a piece of lemon, then sponge with a solution of 1 teaspoon baking soda to ½ a litre of warm water. Rub up with a chamois.

GLACÉ FRUIT

A glacé is a hard, shiny coating made of sugar and water that is applied to fruits to increase their eye and taste appeal. Fruits that are to be glacéed must be perfectly dry, as moisture is fatal to the process. Oranges, cherries, grapes with a bit of the stems left on, prunes, figs and candied peel are among the fruits most easily glacéd.

GLASSWARE
Caring for Glass

■ To clean decanters and small necked bottles which have become stained inside shake a few spoons of uncooked rice and suds inside. A tablespoon of vinegar and fresh tea leaves or warm water with a grated, peeled potato added are also useful cleansers.

■ Glasstoppers which have become jammed can be loosened by dripping in a little warm olive oil on the sides of the stopper. Leave for 30 minutes.

■ When washing valuable, fine glassware, line sink with an old towel.

■ Put a few lemon skins in the rinsing water when washing glassware. The acid from the lemon gives the glass added brilliance.

■ When cleaning glass in picture frames, never use water as moisture could seep through frame edges and stain or spot the picture. Use methylated spirits, as this evaporates quickly. Apply with a paper tissue, then polish with a dry one.

■ Ammonia gives a new sparkle to glassware when washing. Just add a few drops to the rinsing water.

■ For clear glasses, put a small amount of Silica Gel in the cabinet. Musicians keep moisture out of valuable equipment this way.

■ To separate tumblers stuck together, fill the inside one with cold water and place the outer one in warm water. One will contract, the other expand and they will separate easily.

■ Soak discoloured glass baking dishes in a strong solution of borax and water and baked-on stains will quickly disappear.

■ To clean a glass container stained by flowers in water, dissolve one or two Steradent tablets in hot or warm water. Allow to stand inside glass for several hours or overnight. This is also good for cleaning inside wine decanters or stained teapot.

■ To remove marks on glass, use jeweller's rouge. Rub on lightly, then polish over. If scratches are not too deep, Goddard's Plate Powder will remove them. Toothpaste also can be used.

■ To clean glassware, rinse with cold water to which a little vinegar has been added. When washing, add a pinch of baking powder instead of soap.

Cutting Glass Bottles

■ Soak a length of thick string in kerosene and tie tightly around the bottle where you want to cut it through. Light the string with a match. When the string has burnt out, pick up bottle at the bottom with a piece of cloth. Lower bottle upside down into a bucket of water. This should break cleanly at the heated spot.

■ Take a length of fairly stout wire and get someone with strong hands to form one end into a circle, to fit down on to the shoulder of the bottle. Heat the circle in a hot fire or over a flame, put the neck of the bottle into the glowing circle and plunge the lot into cold water. The glass will be cut neatly under the wire. Smooth off any sharp edges.

Making Holes in Glass

To make holes in wine bottles for lamps, use a 6 mm rawplug glass drill. Use a steady pressure and lubricate while drilling with a mixture of 1 block of camphor to half cup of turpentine to stop shattering. Use a wheelbrace and slow speed electric drill. Can be used for glass, pottery and china.

Wiping Up Glass Fragments

■ Use a dampened wad of cotton wool or tissue paper.

Cleaning Bottles

■ Clean old bottles with caustic soda. As this can burn your skin, wear rubber gloves and use a long handled bottle brush. Soak bottles for several days. Often white marks do not come off easily if they are really old and therefore need soaking for several weeks, not days.
■ Fill bottles with broken egg shells and ammonia mixed with water and leave overnight. Repeat process until clean but leave only about a quarter of the mixture in bottle when shaking.
■ Fill bottle with water and add bleach and rice. Leave overnight and shake well next day.
■ Fill bottle with Steradent and leave overnight. When rinsing after treatment, add a few drops ammonia to the water for that sparkle-clean.

GLUE
Make Your Own Glue

■ Put 1 level teaspoon powdered alum in 600 ml of water and bring to the boil. Mix a large cup of plain flour to a smooth paste, using about 1 cup of cold water. Stir into the alum water and continue stirring until mixture is as clear as boiled starch. Stir in few drops of oil of cloves. Strain through wire strainer, bottle in a wide mouthed jar. Line lids with waxed paper. This economical glue keeps well in warm weather. An adhesive giving no discoloration.
■ To make cheap paste for children, boil a cup of water with a dessertspoon of starch for 15 minutes and then stir in half a teaspoon of alum. Bottle the liquid and seal tightly.

When Glue Dries Out

To moisten glue, add a little vinegar.

GOLD
Cleaning Gold Jewellery

■ To clean old gold jewellery, drop the article into undiluted cloudy ammonia for 10 minutes or longer. Rinse under cold water and pat dry with a paper towel. For crevices, an old toothbrush dipped in cloudy ammonia works quite well.
■ Clean jewellery in a solution of detergent and warm water. A mascara brush is helpful in removing dirt from the back of stones.
■ To make an effective polishing cloth, mix two teaspoons of plate powder, 2 dessertspoons cloudy ammonia and 1½ cups of warm water. Soak a flannelette cloth in this mixture until it completely absorbs the liquid. Leave to dry, then polish with a plain flannelette cloth. Use cloth for quick polishing jobs. Can also be used for silver.

■ To clean old gold jewellery like bracelets or pendants, fill a small china cup or basin with methylated spirits. Swirl jewellery around. Gently brush with old soft toothbrush. Remove from spirits and let dry. Rub with soft cloth to shine.

GOLDFISH

Homemade feed for goldfish: sprinkle oatmeal flakes on the water. This will last them several weeks.

GOURDS

To dry gourds or pumpkins, pick when very ripe, late in the afternoon. Gourds should not have been watered for several weeks before picking. Put on cake stands in a warm, dry, shady place indoors. When perfectly dry, either wax polish or paint with clear lacquer.

GRAVY

■ When in a hurry, a little mashed potato will thicken gravy. Mix smoothly.
■ If gravy from a roast is too pale, add a teaspoon of soy sauce or instant coffee. Gives flavour as well as colour.
■ Keep gravy smooth by adding a little salt to the flour before putting in the water.

HAIR

■ Add a few drops of ammonia to the final rinse when washing your hair for that **added shine**.
■ For **dry hair** try a weekly hot oil pack. Heat olive, peanut or almond oil by standing a cup of oil in a saucepan of hot water. Dip your fingertips in oil and vigorously rub into your scalp. Part hair and apply oil right on scalp. Massage for five minutes, then wrap head in a hot towel. Leave hot towel on for five minutes. Shampoo as usual.
■ Here's an **alternative shampoo** to use when the bathroom cabinet is bare. Beat an egg with the juice of a lemon. This gives hair a perfect natural gloss. For fine hair, a beer rinse gives extra body.
■ When **setting hair between shampoos**, wet the plastic rollers instead of your hair. Your hair will dry much more quickly.
■ A good economical **hair-setting lotion**. Dissolve 1 teaspoon gelatine in ½ cup hot water, then mix in 1 teaspoon glycerine. Add two cups hot water. Bottle, then pour mixture as required over hair after shampooing and rinsing. Dry and set in usual way.
■ **Non-greasy Hair Oil:**
Take 100 g bay rum, 50 g pure glycerine, 15 g oil of almonds and a few drops of essence of roses, jasmine or violets. Place all together in a jar and shake well. The mixture can be stored in well-washed spray-type plastic packs and can be sprayed lightly on hair before combing through.

Dandruff Remedies

■ Thoroughly mix 2 tablespoons vinegar, 1 tablespoon castor oil and 1 tablespoon bay rum. Rub scalp thoroughly with solution, leave for 30 minutes, shampoo as usual. Add 2 tablespoons vinegar to the last rinsing water.

■ Another good dandruff remover. Massage shaving cream into the scalp. Rinse well, using cold water for the last rinse.

HAM
How to Cure Hams

To each ham of about 6.5 kg, allow 2.2 kg bay salt, 226 g common salt, 28 g black pepper, 57 g saltpetre. Powder these well together, lay ham in mixture for 4 days, turning and rubbing meat every day. Then add 680 g treacle to each ham, let lie in that for 4 weeks, turning each day. Take out, soak in water for 24 hours, hang up to dry.

HANDBAGS

■ To clean patterned leather handbags, use a soft nail brush wrapped in a lint-free dust cloth. Rub vaseline into the bag and brush. Then use another cloth in the same way as a buffer. Keeps the leather beautifully soft. Also good for leather shoes..

■ To clean doeskin, apply Faulding Solyptol liquid with a soft cloth, gently wipe over surface, then wipe carefully with a clean cloth.

HAND LOTIONS
Three Do-It-Yourself Lotions

■ Mix 1 dessertspoon each of honey, olive oil, lemon juice and glycerine. Keeps well in a corked bottle.

■ For a lotion for chapped hands, grate or flake a cake of camphor, add one cup methylated spirits, and a small bottle of glycerine. Put all in a bottle and shake well until camphor is dissolved.

■ One cup toilet soap pieces (not laundry soap), half cup lemon juice, 2 teaspoons perfume such as lavender, 1 dessertspoon olive or almond oil, 16 g glycerine, 6 ml menthol crystals, 560 ml pure methylated spirit. Melt soap, strain on lemon juice, add all other ingredients and store in bottle. Shake well before using.

HANDS

■ Clean garden soiled hands by putting a little sugar and olive oil into your palms. Rub well. Removes all grime, softens hands.

■ For brittle or flaking fingernails, mix 2 level teaspoons gelatine into half glass of fruit juice or cold water, or a mixture of both. Drink at once. Repeat daily for 6 weeks or longer.

■ Rub your hands with a slice of lemon to remove onion or garlic odour.

■ To remove wood stains from hands, wash in lemon juice. A final rinse with diluted household bleach will also assist: 1 part bleach to 3 parts water. Sugar soap, available from hardware shops, is also effective.

■ Here's a third solution for wood-stained hands. First wash hands in hot water, the hotter the better. Next partly dry hands, leaving them very damp and hot. As soon as possible, apply a few drops of baby oil, olive or any similar bland oil. Rub well into hands. Wash hands again in very hot water. Depending on the stains, more than one treatment may be necessary.

■ Nicotine stains on fingers can be removed easily by rubbing with nail polish remover.

HATS

■ **Felt hats** will clean like new if rubbed all over with very fine sandpaper. Then brush the same way as the grain.

■ To clean **straw hats** combine juice of 1 lemon, ¼ teaspoon epsom salts, 1 teaspoon cooking salt and a little lukewarm water. Rub over hat.

■ To clean a **bowling hat** with green under its brim, place hat in a bucket of warm water and add about a quarter cup of laundry liquid. Let soak for an hour or so, then rinse but do not squeeze. Rinse well then add liquid starch to last water. Place hat over a basin to fit crown and put on a towel in the shade outside to dry. When dry, iron the hat and shape it whatever way you like. Comes up like new.

■ For **panama hats**, beat together the white of an egg, juice of ½ a lemon and 1 teaspoon salt. Apply to hat with brush. Wipe off with damp cloth and put outside, not in the sun, to dry. This will clean, stiffen and whiten hat.

■ Remove band of the **panama hat** and sponge hat with a solution of 28 ml epsom salts dissolved in 568 ml hot water. Use the solution when it is warm, and do not soak the straw. Leave to dry thoroughly, then cover stained parts with hydrogen peroxide and dry in the sun. Repeat the peroxide treatments, drying each time in the sun until hat is evenly cleaned all over.

■ To clean a **white felt bowling hat**, use carpet shampoo. Let it dry and brush with stiff brush. Fine emery paper will also clean a white felt hat. Rub with paper, then rub over lightly with block magnesia and leave a day before brushing.

■ Prevent men's light-coloured **felt hats** from becoming soiled through use of hair oil. Place a strip of blotting paper inside the leather lining.

HEADACHES

Headaches are often cured by taking the juice of a lemon and half a teaspoon of bicarbonate soda. Mix and drink while fizzing.

HEATERS

To clean Vulcan Oil Heater candles, turn heater on high for 10 minutes. Candles will glow red and this automatically cleans them.

HICCOUGH CURE

Take 1 teaspoon brown sugar moistened with white vinegar. Another cure which works for some people: drink a glass of water with nostrils closed, breathe out deeply and stop breathing for a count of 10.

ICE CREAM

■ **Caramel Ice Cream:**
Add 50 g caramels melted in a saucepan over boiling water to ice cream recipe after final beating, then freeze as usual.

■ **Party Ice Cream:**
Cut up coloured gum jubes and fold them through the ice cream while soft. Use scissors dipped in hot water to cut the jubes.

ICE CUBES
Stop 'Em Sticking

■ Rub the outside of ice cube trays with glycerine and they will never stick to the fridge. Wipe dry before applying glycerine on a cloth.

■ To prevent ice cubes sticking after taking them from trays, squirt cubes all over with soda water from a siphon. Place in poly bags and store in freezer.

■ Plastic ice cube trays are flexible and ice cubes pop out easily. Running water over the ice trays wets the surface of the ice, causes cubes to stick together and makes them difficult to use.

Party Ice

If cubes are for a party, a few drips of angostura in each tray prior to freezing will give pink cubes for children's drinks,

punches and pink gins and add a final touch to party drinks. Is non-alcoholic.

ICING

■ Try this unusual jam icing for a plain cake. Bring four tablespoons red jam slowly to the boil, boil for one minute. Pour over stiffly beaten egg white and beat until mixture is stiff.

■ Make a crunchy butterscotch icing by beating the white of an egg until light and frothy but not stiff. Add 1 cup brown sugar, a pinch salt and ½ teaspoon vanilla. Spread over top of cake before baking.

Handy Hints

■ A few drops of vinegar added to icing will make it set in half the time. Does not affect the flavour.

■ Icing for a chocolate cake will not moisten on the cake if you add a teaspoon of cornflour when mixing the icing sugar and cocoa.

■ Add a dessertspoon of condensed milk when making icing. Will be firm but soft, and will not crack.

No Sweat Plastic Icing

To prevent plastic icing sweating in humid weather, buy silica gel crystals. Put in small containers around cake or give cake the dry heat treatment by placing a heater on one side of the cake and a fan on low speed on the other side. Shut the door. The crystals change colour as they absorb moisture and should be placed in warm oven to dry out. They then retain their original colour and can be used again.

Icing Substitute

Put some dry powdered milk in a basin. Press out all lumps, add one spoonful condensed milk and mix well. Add evaporated milk to get the right consistency, then a pinch of salt and flavouring.

Icing Bag

Make an instant icing bag from aluminium foil. Twist to a cone, shape and snip off a tiny piece at the point.

INDIGESTION

Indigestion from a spicy meal is often prevented if you add a little ground ginger to the ingredients. Ideal for stews and rissoles.

INDOOR PLANTS

■ Good tonic for indoor plants and bulbs is drop of olive oil once a week. Makes them grow faster and gives leaves a glossier green.
■ Tie a large plastic bag over a small plant in a pot to **aid early growth**.
■ Add a handful of foam rubber filling when potting plants. Mix it in with the soil. This saves watering more than a couple of times a week.

INSECTS

Get rid of insect pests by sprinkling borax powder or boric acid around appliances and baseboards.

IRONING
Easy Ironing Tips

■ Iron difficult things like shirts and pyjamas first. They will seem to get done more quickly and make the rest of the ironing more of a pleasure.
■ Set up ironing board in a pleasant spot, turn on radio or your favourite records, even TV. Sit down to work, don't stand, adjusting board to a comfortable working height.
■ Work with long, smooth strokes instead of short, abrupt ones and save yourself effort and energy.
■ To give a professional finish to ironing, wrap a piece of beeswax in a small square flannel and run quickly over the surface of iron when hot. Polish with a clean cloth.
■ Soap rubbed on the inside of trouser creases before pressing will keep the crease in longer and look better.
■ Before pressing trousers, put a little starch in the water used to dampen the pressing cloth. This makes creases stay sharp.
■ Put brown paper over trousers when pressing to prevent a shine from iron.

IRONS

For brown stains on an iron, rub with a cut lemon when cold. Wipe over with a damp cloth, polish with a dry one.
■ Clean inside a **steam iron** by filling with a mixture of 2 dessertspoons white wine vinegar and 2 dessertspoons distilled water. Put the hot iron on a cake cooler covered with old linen.
■ A sticky iron can be made to operate smoothly again if run back and forth, while hot, over a sheet of paper on which salt has been sprinkled generously.
■ Rust marks on an electric iron can be removed by rubbing with petroleum jelly. Leave for 2 days, then clean off with ammonia.

IVORY

■ To clean ivory, apply whiting moistened with turpentine or soak in water and borax. Do not use soap as this causes yellowness. Rub discoloured dominos with a cloth dipped in methylated spirits or dampened with eau de cologne. Ivory dominos can also be brightened by covering with a paste of lemon juice and french chalk. Leave on for 3 hours or overnight. Remove with cloth wrung out in hot water. A poultice of peroxide and whiting is also effective. Allow to dry before removing, then brush off. You can also try whiting and lemon juice. Moisten whiting and apply with soft old toothbrush. Leave on a few minutes. Add a little borax to some rinsing water and use this to brush off whiting, or rinse by soaking in borax and water. However, for valuable ivory pieces, consult professionals.

JAM
Basic Jam Making Rules

■ **Adding sugar**. Simmer jam before adding sugar. Boil quickly as soon as sugar has dissolved.

■ **Scum**. Do not remove scum until jam is almost at setting point. Most of the froth formed in the early stages will boil clear.

■ **Jam making faults**. If runny, jam may not have been boiled long enough, or may be lacking in sugar, or may have been made with too much sugar. If syrupy, jam may have been boiled too long.

■ **Jelling**. Add lemon juice, citric or tartaric acid to improve jelling of jams which do not set well.

■ **Setting point**. Test for 'set' by placing a teaspoonful of jam on a cold plate. Cool rapidly and test to see whether a skin has formed which wrinkles when plate is tilted. If not, continue to boil.

Tips for Tip-top Jam

■ **Bubbles in Marmalade**. There are two causes of air bubbles in marmalade: 1. Marmalade was allowed to cool too much before being poured into jars. If cooled too much, bubbles can form on pouring and will be trapped through the jam. Jars should also be hot. Or: 2. The marmalade was poured too slowly into the jars. Air bubbles can be eliminated by tipping marmalade back into a saucepan, heating but not boiling, then returning to the heated jars.

■ **Why Jams Crystallise**. Using too much sugar or over-boiling can cause jam to crystallise. Also occurs if jam is boiled too rapidly before sugar is added. The jam should not be stirred too much when boiling or be left uncovered for too long. Most jams require comparatively long and slow cooking before the sugar is added, and rapid boiling afterwards. If the jam is not too stiff, it can be re-boiled for a few minutes with extra water and lemon juice.

■ **Easy Covers for Jam Jars**. Boil a little sago with a dessertspoon of vinegar. Rub this over both sides of sheets of brown paper. Cut to desired size and press down over jam jars. This forms an airtight covering and is inexpensive.

■ **Prevent Mildew Forming on Jam**. Mildew may be caused by using wet, cold jars, covering them when neither hot nor cold; using insufficient sealing when covering, or by storing the jam in a damp place. Adding insufficient sugar or too

much water can also promote mildew, as can insufficient boiling or storage in a hot place. If clear seals are used, dampen them with pure white vinegar. This makes the covers tight. Store all jams on the lowest shelf in the pantry, where the temperature is cooler. Sterilise bottles in slow oven and use while still warm.

■ For **musty smells**, add three teaspoons bicarb of soda to 1 litre warm water. Cover jars and leave about a day. Rinse thoroughly.

■ Sometimes smells clinging to rubber rings inside jam lids are impossible to fully remove. Often better to cover lid with foil before sealing.

■ **Wash** jars in hot soapy water, rinse, turn upside down to dry, then add a few drops of vanilla and water. Leave a while, then rinse.

■ **To Remove Stubborn Lids:** Immerse bottle or jar upside down in hot water. The heat causes the lid to expand and release.

■ **Easy Slide Screw Tops:** Rub a little olive oil inside the edges of screw-top jars when bottling fruit. This prevents rust; tops are quick and easy to unscrew.

■ **Mince** melon or pineapple for jam. It's quicker than cutting the fruit and makes a more even mixture.

■ Juice of a lemon added to almost any jam when cooking makes for **faster jelling** and improves the colour.

■ Allow **marmalade** to cool for 10 minutes before bottling. This allows the shreds to be well distributed.

■ If bottling jams for fetes or stalls, put a coloured paper patty cake container under lid. Makes an **attractive seal**.

■ See recipes under *Cooking*.

JARS
To Clean Smelly Jars

■ Half fill jars with cold water which contains 1 tablespoon dry mustard. Shake, stand for 20 minutes, then rinse thoroughly.

■ Fill jars with warm water containing 1 tablespoon of tea leaves and 1 tablespoon vinegar. Stand 3 to 4 hours, then shake out and rinse.

JEWELLERY

A piece of camphor in the box with your chunky jewellery will stop tarnishing and keeps the stones bright.

JUNKET

When making junket, instead of using sugar, melt 2 or 3 marshmallows in the hot milk. When milk is warm, add to junket tablet in the usual way.

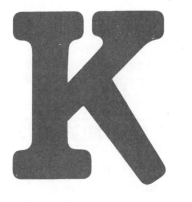

KEROSENE LAMPS

Most lamp problems, like smell and smoke, arise from two sources. Kerosene comes in 2 varieties: lighting kerosene and industrial kerosene. When buying from a garage, insist that you get lighting kero, and not the other variety from their 200 litre drum. Lighting kero rarely smokes or gives off a pungent smell. The second important task is trimming the wick. Extend flat wick to a point well beyond the surface of the wick holder. If large flame is required, trim wick with sharp scissors straight across. This gives a maximum flame. If an adjustable spear point flame is required, trim wick in a fairly sharp curve.

KETTLES

■ To **clean a kettle**, boil 2 teaspoons cream of tartar in 1 100 ml of water in the kettle for a few minutes, then rinse thoroughly. Add a few clean pebbles during the boil to break up thick depositis.

■ To clean **furred kettles** boiled on stove, fill with water and add 2 teaspoons of borax, boil for about 20 minutes. Scrape off any fur remaining and rinse out thoroughly.

■ To prevent corrosion in **cast iron kettle**, put 2 or 3 glass marbles in bottom of kettle. The movement of the marbles in boiling water will cut out corrosion.

■ Smear the **corroded area** of your kettle with vaseline and leave an hour or two before adding 1 cup baking soda and filling the kettle with clear water. Bring to boil and boil slowly for a few minutes, then set aside and leave overnight. Next day a metal pot scourer will remove any remaining corrosion. Rinse kettles really well with hot water before using.

■ To **clean electric kettles** wipe exterior of kettle with damp cloth or sponge as necessary. Do not immerse in water. To clean inside the kettle, half fill it with 1.3 litres of water. Add 30 ml white vinegar, plug in the kettle and switch on. Allow to boil a total of 10 to 15 minutes, or for auto-boil model hold the spout cover open so that it will not cut out. Switch off, remove plug, empty kettle then rinse at least 3 times to remove all dislodged particles.

KNITTING

■ To be sure the cast off row is not too tight, use a needle one size larger for this row.

■ Press finished work between two sheets of brown paper instead of a damp cloth. Use a warm iron. This will not flatten the pattern.

■ When knitting socks, knit shirring elastic in the tops with the yarn for about 5 or 6 rows.

LACE
Washing Lovely Old Lace

Wash in warm soapy water by squeezing and kneading. Rinse in warm water. Use gum water to stiffen after washing. You need 125 g gum arabic to half a litre of water. Dissolve gum in hot water. Strain and bottle. Add to final rinsing water, using 1 to 3 tablespoons to each half litre of water, according to stiffness required. Roll lace in a towel until almost dry. Iron on wrong side over a towel or pad to make pattern stand out.

LAMINATED SURFACES

■ Keep laminated surfaces shining by rubbing over with methylated spirits on a soft cloth.
■ To remove **Superglue** from laminex, sponge with amyl acetate, then wash with warm water and washing-up detergent added. Rinse with warm water. Repeat if necessary. Amyl acetate available from chemists.
■ For **faded** formica, wipe over with warm soapy water. Dry off immediately and then apply a little linseed oil on a soft clean cloth. Rub on to surface and then give a final polish with Windex for a great shine. Wiping laminated surfaces over with soda water also gives a brilliant shine.
■ To remove **tea stains** from laminex use

ordinary bleach. Just pour a small amount on old rag and wipe all over bench. Leave a short time, then wash off. Bleach will remove most stains from laminex without causing any harm to the original colour.

LAMINGTONS

Add a little rum to the icing mixture when making lamingtons. Gives a special flavour and they are not so sweet.
■ See recipes under *Cooking*.

LAMPSHADES

Wax parchment lampshades to make dusting easier. This also works with venetian blinds and your telephone. Soiled parchment shades can be cleaned like this: dissolve a large handful of starch in about 280 ml of cold water. Rub firmly, but carefully, into shade with a household sponge (not too wet). Rinse by squeezing out sponge in cold water. Stand shade on side while cleaning; put back on lamp to dry. If very dirty, use more starch.

LAVENDER
Drying Lavender

■ Pick lavender heads just as they are about to burst into flower. Lay out on trays and let dry in the sun, or a light airy room, turning occasionally.
■ Pick lavender in dry weather, hang in bunches, upside down, with a paper bag tied round the flower heads. Flowers will drop into the bag when they are dry. The addition of a little dried thyme and grated dried lemon rind, about ½ level teaspoon of each to 1 cupful of lavender, will add body to the perfume.

Fresh Idea

Put a little dried lavender into hems of the curtains. As breeze blows and curtains sway, the scent of lavender will fill the room.

LEATHER

Remove stains from leather by using warm water and vinegar, then restore polish by rubbing hard with a cloth dipped in raw linseed oil.

LEMONS
Storing Lemons

■ Be sure the lemons are just ripe and you leave a stalk on each one. Rub glycerine all over lemons, then cover each one separately with aluminium foil. Keep in a dry place with a little space between each lemon.

■ Put a layer of dry sand in a container, then a layer of lemons. Keep them apart. Then another layer of dry sand covering the lemons, continuing the process, finishing with the dry sand layer. They will last for months treated this way.

■ After picking lemons with a little stalk on each, rub well with vaseline or petroleum jelly to clog the pores. Wrap individually in tissue paper. Store in a cool place. Will keep for months. Be sure to scrub well and wash thoroughly before using.

■ Lemons will keep indefinitely if candle grease is smeared over them. Melt candle and rub wax over peel. When ready to use, crack the wax and it will come off easily.

Magic — More Juice!

Warm lemons before squeezing for much more juice.

Preserving Lemon Juice

Place juice in plastic ice cube trays and freeze. Store in plastic containers or plastic bags in your freezer. Use when required.

LETTUCE
Revive Limp Lettuce

Add 2 teaspoons sugar to 1100 ml water when soaking. Will soon be crisp again. Another way is to add juice of half a lemon to the water.

Lettuce must not only be crisp but dry. Wash carefully leaf by leaf, shake off water, then pat leaf by leaf with clean cloth or paper towel to really remove water before putting in crisper box in fridge.

Fresher for Longer

Lettuce keeps fresh longer if you add a piece of paper towel, or anything similar, which will absorb moisture in the bottom of the crisper.

LILAC

Do not break the blooms off the bush; remove them with suitable cutters. Then place the end of the stalks on a firm object and hammer flat. Strip all leaves off the stalk as the leaves take the water, not the bloom. Some people believe in dipping stalk ends in hot water, but just placing blooms straight into a container of water is usually successful. Lilac blooms absorb a lot of water over several days, so the more water given, the longer the blooms last.

LINEN

■ To remove stains from stored white linen, use Rit Colour Remover soak in an enzyme soaking solution. Wet article first, them immerse in the cold pre-wash soak. Must be cold because enzymes are destroyed by heat. The enzymes will absorb any bacteria that are present.

■ When washing **tea-stained linen**, rub a little glycerine into each stain. When washed should be white.

■ Remove stubborn **rust stains** or discoloration from linen by dampening them and rubbing with a little tartaric acid. Put in the sun. Repeat process until stains disappear. Another method is to boil in a solution of 570 ml of water and 2 teaspoons of cream of tartar. Rinse well and allow to dry.

■ Unbleached **sheets** should be washed for the first time in a copper with 2 tablespoons of turpentine. Boil well and they'll whiten at once.

■ To remove **mildew**, soak article in kerosene, then roll up and leave for 24 hours. Rinse well and wash as usual. Moisten mildew stains with lemon juice and salt. Dry in sun, wash as usual. Ammonia and whiting mixed in a paste will also remove mildew.

■ To wash **flannelette sheets** without pilling, wash them separately from other items in a tub of warm water with this mixture: small handful lathered soap flakes, 300 ml methylated spirits, 2 dessertspoons eucalyptus. Push and swish the sheets about without rubbing. Do not rinse, hand wring lightly and hang out, preferably on a breezy day. There will be no piling and sheets will smell wonderful.

■ For the first few times when washing flannelette sheets, do them separately from other linens as the fluff covers other pieces and is difficult to remove. Then soak the sheets in salt and a tablespoon of vinegar overnight. Next day rinse in clean water with ½ a cup of epsom salts. Hang on line to dry. This will prevent piling.

■ To prevent **stored linen** going grey, buy blue coloured, acid-free (repeat acid-free) tissue paper at stationers or newsagents. Place a sheet of the tissue between each article, and finish by wrapping the lot in the blue paper.

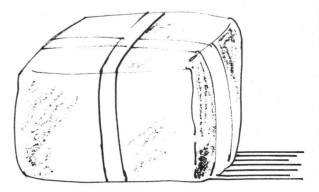

■ Remove **tea and coffee stains** from tablecloths by rubbing salt into the cloth after rinsing with cold water. Freshly spilled coffee or tea usually will not leave a stain after this exercise.

■ For **old stains**, soak tablecloths for half an hour before washing in a solution of 2 tablespoons liquid bleach to 4.5 litres of water for white cotton or linen cloths. Use half-strength for coloured ones. After soaking, wash as usual. For bad stains you may have to wash like this two or three times.

■ Treat **new coffee stains** with this warm borax solution: 15 g borax to 300 ml of water. Rinse and launder. For **old stains**, sponge with cold water, rub glycerine in well, leave half an hour, rinse with clean warm water. For **tea stains**, treat immediately by pouring boiling water through from a height. Sponge coloured cloths with warm water and borax solution: 30 g to 600 ml. Rub old stains on whites with lemon juice, hang in strong sunlight.

■ To remove **yellow spots** from stored linen, use 2 tablespoons borax to 2.3 litres of lukewarm water and soak articles overnight. Then wash in the ordinary way next day. This method was very successful on a 50 year old christening gown.

80

LINO

■ When **old lino** is shabby, go over floor with a flannel cloth dipped in a mixture of 1 part turpentine to 2 parts olive oil. Shake well before using.

■ **Brown marks** can be removed from lino by rubbing with kerosene and steel wool. Wash afterwards with detergent.

■ To remove brown **shoe polish** from vinyl lino, use Ajax all-purpose solvent cleaner called Spray N Wipe. A little kerosene and steel wool, followed by a wash with detergent and warm water is also usually effective. If not successful, try a little lighter fluid or a cloth moistened with eucalyptus oil.

■ To remove **furniture dents** in lino, simply melt a wax crayon of the same colour as the lino and press firmly into the dent or hole. Leave to harden, then polish.

LOGS
Logs from Old Newspapers

Boil 2½ litres water in a kerosene tin, adding 1 kg washing soda. When dissolved, put newspapers in boiling mixture and boil 10 minutes, prodding continuously with a stick. Allow to cool, mould into balls about the size of a tennis ball, squeezing each as tightly as possible. Put on rack or table to dry. When dry, start fire with a few chips of wood and a few brickettes and each log will burn for nearly an hour.

LOUNGE CHAIRS

To clean fabric lounge and chairs, mix enough soap flakes in hot water to make plenty of frothy suds. Using a soft cloth slightly rub stains and dirt using only the froth, dry using another cloth. Do not use the water. Repeat if necessary. Powder upholstery cleaners are also effective. Rub in with a towel, leave for 15 minutes and

vacuum off. Another method: sprinkle with powdered magnesia and work in well. Leave several hours, then brush out with a soft brush.

LUGGAGE

Before storing luggage after a holiday, add a cake of camphor to each case. Will smell fresh and keep linings safe from pests.

MACADAMIA NUTS
How to Roast

Thoroughly dried nuts are tasty and ready to eat. However, if you prefer them roasted, pre-heat oven to 120°C. Place nut meat in a shallow pan, no more than two nuts deep to assure good air circulation. Do not mix nut meat of different sizes, as small pieces will scorch. Roast nuts 40 to 50 minutes, stirring occasionally. Remove from oven as soon as they start to brown as this process continues after removal from oven. Sprinkle with salt. The nuts should have oozed sufficient oil to make the salt cling, but you can add a dab of butter or neutral flavoured oil. Serve nuts hot or cool. Store in tightly sealed jar in fridge or freezer.

How to Crack Macadamia Nuts

Vice-grips are the most efficient crackers for macadamia nuts. They use leverage to

produce great pressure at the jaws, which do not suddenly close and crush the nut as pliers and hammers do. Hold nuts in the vice and wind handle gently. Soaking the shells overnight softens them, making cracking easier. Placing nuts in the oven for a few minutes also aids cracking.

MAHOGANY

For a high polish on mahogany, rub with lemon oil, pour alcohol on soft cheesecloth and rub on wood. Will come up gleaming.

MARBLE

■ To remove rust on **white marble**, dilute 1 part of oxalic acid with 10 parts of alcohol. Cover the spot with a pad of gauze saturated with the mixture and let it stand for 15 to 30 minutes. Wash off with water containing ammonia rinse and wipe dry.

■ To remove rust on **coloured marble** cover the spot with a heavy application of common salt and moisten with fresh lemon juice. Give ample time to remove the spot, then wash the marble with water containing sal soda, rinse and wipe dry.

■ To remove **oil and grease spots** from marble, cover the spot with a heavy application of starch or whiting and saturate with naphtha, benzol or alcohol. Let stand for several hours, even overnight. Repeat if necessary. Wash with water containing sal soda, rinse and wipe dry.

■ To remove stains on **black marble** mix equal amounts of baking soda, whiting and common salt with water to the consistency of thick cream. Pour this mixture over the marble and let stand until all stains are removed. Wash with water and soap, rinse and wipe dry.

Marble Polish

Polish marble by covering the surface with water and sprinkling with whiting or pumice. Tack a piece of felt to a block of wood and rub from the centre outward in circular motions until the desired polish is obtained. Do not use a rotary power polisher for this purpose, it will blemish the surface with faint circles. A flat, vibrating power sander with felt attached does a good job and does not leave any blemishes. If there are only small circles or spots that require polishing, there is no need to go over the entire surface.

MARSHMALLOWS
Soften Them Up

Marshmallows which have hardened will be soft and fresh again if you put them in a plastic bag, seal well and dip in hot water.

Birthday Marshmallows

Marshmallows make good candle holders on birthday cakes, saves wax running on to the cake.

■ See recipes under *Cooking*.

MASCARA

To soften mascara, immerse container of mascara in a mug or jar of hot water. Leave a few minutes before using. Never fails, is easier to apply and mascara goes further.

MASSAGE
Two Massage Liniments

■ To make old-fashioned massage liniment, you need 10 g each spirits of wine and spirits of turpentine, 2 small blocks of camphor, 1 whole egg and enough vinegar to cover egg to dissolve shell. Wash egg and place in cup of vinegar until all egg shell is dissolved. Crush camphor well. Break skin from egg, remove skin and mix all ingredients together including whole egg and vinegar. Bottle and shake well before use.

■ One cup each vinegar and turps, 1 beaten egg, 1 cake grated camphor, 1 teaspoon DD eucalyptus, 2 tablespoons olive oil. Place all ingredients into a bottle, shake well. This liniment improves with age, keeps on the bathroom shelf for years.

MAYONNAISE

To improve flavour and double the quantity, beat up an egg white to a stiff froth and add it to mayonnaise.

MEAT LOAF

When making a meat loaf for dinner, bake a few small ones in paper patty pans to include in tomorrow's lunch.

MERINGUE

To make meringue crisp and fluffy, add a quarter teaspoon baking powder while beating. For a soft centre, add a few drops of vinegar to meringue mixture.

MILK

■ To prevent boil-overs, butter around the inside top of the saucepan. The milk stays put.
■ Sour milk is a good buttermilk substitute. To make it sour, add a tablespoon of vinegar or lemon juice to a cup of fresh milk, or milk that is a day or two old.
■ To prevent skim milk burning a saucepan, spray with Spray and Cook before putting milk into pan. Another method is to grease the inside of the pan with butter.

MILK PUDDINGS

Milk puddings are made richer and creamier by using evaporated milk with 2 parts water.

MINCED MEAT

To improve the flavour of minced meat while cooking, add 1 teaspoon each vinegar and sugar for each 500 g of meat.

MINT

Dip mint in vinegar before chopping for mint sauce and it will keep its bright green colour.

MIRRORS

■ For dull mirrors, pour boiling water over used tea leaves, strain off the liquid and bottle. Dampen a soft piece of flannel with this for cleaning.
■ Old nylons are useful for polishing mirrors and windows. They leave no lint and give glass a high gloss.
■ Prevent bathroom mirrors fogging up by rubbing with a cloth dipped in equal amounts of glycerine and methylated spirits, then polish.

MOHAIR

Mohair garments will be soft and fluffy if washed in shampoo.

MONSTERA DELICIOSA
Preparing Fruit for Eating

Ripe fruitlets should be lifted off with a fork, then thoroughly washed in a strainer under running water to remove the many small black hairs present, thus avoiding severe irritation to the mouth. After removing the ripe fruitlets, the remainder of the core can be wrapped in paper for a few more days to ripen. When removing the fruitlets from the core, extreme care must be used to avoid taking any green or unripe fruitlets, as these will cause a very unpleasant irritation in the mouth and throat.

MOSQUITOES
Goodbye Mozzies

A few drops of spirits of camphor from chemists on a lump of sugar will keep mosquitoes away if placed on bedside table. A pot of basil on the windowsill or outside on the terrace will deter mozzies too.

Goodbye Itch

Take sting and itch from mosquito bites by applying vinegar mixed with bicarbonate of soda.

MOSS

Moss can be removed from a brick path by painting over with methylated spirits.

MOTHS
Repel Those Moths

■ Moths will not come near drawers which have been wiped over with a strong ammonia solution.
■ Keep moths away by dropping a few cloves or sprinkling epsom salts in corners of wardrobes, cupboards, under carpets.
■ To keep moths out of the pantry, get rid of anything in the cupboards that you suspect may be infested like barley, cornflour and so on. Don't just throw the stuff out, burn if possible, or wrap in paper and spray bundles before putting in garbage bin.

Moths Love These Foods

Food like barley, rice and rolled oats can be spread on trays in hot oven for 20 minutes or so, then cooled and stored in glass or plastic containers with tight-fitting lids, keeping them safe from moths. Keep an eye on packets of dried fruits; these are often forgotten if not used frequently.

MUSHROOMS
How to Store Mushrooms

■ Mushrooms are naturally at their best in food value and flavour when eaten fresh but they do store well. As mushrooms have a high water content, the secret is to store them so they have little chance of evaporation. Place in a container with a tightly fitting lid, or seal in foil or plastic film and store in refrigerator.
■ Large quantities may be stored well in an open tray or vegetable container in fridge if a moistened paper towel or open-weave cloth is placed over the surface.
■ Freeze mushrooms like this. Do not wash or clean at all. Place in waxed or freezer plastic containers with sealing lids. Freeze quickly and keep in freezer shelf of fridge for 2 to 3 weeks, or a full size freezer for 3 to 4 weeks. Use without thawing.

■ Or sauté mushrooms, either whole or sliced in butter for half the usual cooking time. Pack in waxed or freezer plastic containers, seal and freeze quickly. These will keep 3 to 4 weeks on a freezer shelf, 2 to 3 months in full size freezer. When required for use, simply remove seal and thaw, then prepare as required.

Drying Mushrooms

Mushrooms should be very fresh. Peel if you prefer, or wipe clean with a damp cloth. Spread mushrooms on trays, or thread them on fine string with a knot between each to prevent them touching each other. Dry at a temperature not higher than 50°C until they are dry and shrivelled. Pack in jars or bottles. Store in dry place. The mushrooms on a string can be hung up in a cool, dry place.

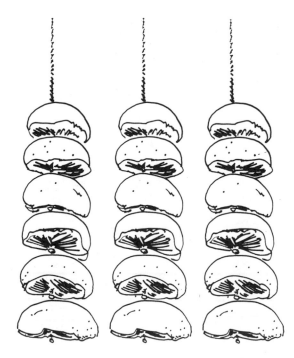

NAIL POLISH

■ To restore hardened nail polish add nail polish remover to polish, allow to penetrate in closed bottle, shake vigorously and let stand until properly mixed. This will soften polish. Add polish remover to your own discretion until you can apply polish smoothly to nails.
■ Clear nail polish is excellent for painting over medicine bottle labels to prevent smearing. Also good over addresses on parcels to be posted on wet days and for coating the back of metal necklets or bracelets so that the jewellery won't leave dark marks on the skin.

NAPPY RASH

Home-made ointment for nappy rash. Mix equal parts of olive oil and zinc ointment together. Keep in a screw-top jar. Apply to baby's skin, no powder needed. Ointment heals the rash, olive oil soothes, and wet nappies will not sting. Line nappy with tissues as this ointment stains.

NICKEL

Nickel fittings will sparkle if rubbed over daily with a dry cloth moistened with methylated spirits.

NYLON

■ Restore **discoloured nylon** by soaking for 10 minutes in 1.1 litres hot water, 2 tablespoons methylated spirits, 1 teaspoon ammonia. After soaking, wash in soapy water, rinse. Another useful method: soak nylon in warm water with a dessertspoon of bicarbonate of soda, then wash as usual.

■ Clean collars of grubby **nylon raincoats** with a little liquid hair shampoo.

■ For nylon **shirt collars**, wet both sides with raw starch then iron with a soft cloth over the collar. Be careful iron is not too hot. Makes nylon shirt collars sit properly.

■ To remove **mildew** on nylon shower curtains, soak in solution of 5 litres cold water, half cup bleach and 1 tablespoon vinegar until mildew disappears.

OCTOPUS
Simmered Octopus

To cook octopus, clean and cut into small pieces. Place in saucepan, cover with white wine, add a nob of butter or margarine, simmer until completely cooked. Drain and serve with salt and pepper.

Fried Octopus

Remove tentacles and clean by cutting through the body and removing the internal section. Skin octopus and lay aside the white flesh that remains, slice. Heat oil until very hot and fry octopus for about 5 minutes.

ODOURS
Banish Smells from Plastic Containers

■ Fill container with warm soapy water and add one tablespoon bicarbonate of soda, more if container is large. Leave overnight turning occasionally, repeat if necessary.

■ Cram container full of damp newspapers and leave for several hours.

■ Fill container with cold water and add malt vinegar. Leave for several hours.

■ Fill container with cold water and vanilla essence. Leave for several hours. If any smell remains, put the container in direct sunlight for an hour.

■ Always rinse containers with cold water before washing, as warm or hot water causes odours to remain in container.

■ See also entries like *Books, Clothes,* etc.

Urine Odour

To remove urine odour from pyjamas, soak in Napisan, then wash in usual washing powder with disinfectant added. Then add disinfectant and a fabric softener to final rinse. All odours will then be eradicated. Dry in the open air, in sun if possible.

Shoe Smells

To remove odours from shoes, sprinkle bicarbonate of soda thickly into the shoes, making sure the powder reaches the very tips, then leave for several days. Shake out and air shoes. All odour will have gone. Bicarbonate of soda can be left in shoes when they are not being worn to keep them smelling fresh.

The Smell of an Oily Rag

To remove oil smell from clothing, add a dessertspoon of eucalyptus to the soap powder in washing machine. This removes oil and oil smell. May have to be repeated if smell is very bad.

Tobacco Taints

■ To get rid of tobacco smoke smells in a room, put a little soda in a jar and sprinkle it with a few drops of ammonia and 3 or 4 drops of oil of lavender. Add a few tablespoons of boiling water and leave uncovered in the room to give off a clean, refreshing odour.

■ Mix a few tablespoons of ammonia in water in an old cup or small bowl and leave to stand overnight. Freshen stale-smelling cupboards in the same way.

■ Put ⅓ to ½ cup of brown vinegar in room depending on size and how many people smoking. Also works for smelly cupboards.

■ Dampen a towel with diluted vinegar and wave throughout the room.

■ Freshen a tobacco-tainted room with perfume. Burn small quantity of eau-de-cologne on a saucer or put a few drops of lavender water or similar in a glass of boiling water. Dab some perfume on a light globe. When light is on, heat releases the aroma. A dish of pot-pourri mixture also gives a beautiful perfume.

Meaty Smells

Immerse meat in water mixed with bicarbonate of soda. Takes out smell immediately.

Ugh! Brussel Sprouts

To prevent odour when cooking brussel sprouts, cook in half water and half milk. Not only prevents odour but gives a delicious flavour to the sprouts as well. Adding 2 or 3 stalks of fresh parsley also minimises smell. Can be lifted out when cooked or served with the vegetables for extra flavour and goodness.

Goodbye Musty Odours

To remove the musty smell from a house which has been closed up, burn a small quantity of eau-de-cologne in a saucer.

Ugh! Strong Cat Smells

Buy a bottle of Nilodor from chemist, sprinkle a few drops in each room or sprinkle few drops on cotton wool and place the wads around in each room. All nasty cat smells will soon disappear. This can also be used for all sorts of odours in cupboards, garbage cans, hospital rooms.

Push Paint Smell Out

To remove paint smells from a freshly painted room, place a bowl of water containing a chopped onion in the room. If you place a bowl or pail of water in the room all day, renewing water every 3 hours, this will also absorb paint odours.

OLIVES
Preserved Olives

Make a strong brine, about 500 g salt to 4.5 litres water. Be sure that green olives are fresh, plump and unbruised. Wipe olives, soak in brine for 7 days then remove and pack in jars. Pour brine into a pan and boil, remove scum, when clear add 1 teaspoon brown sugar dissolved in 4.5 litres of water. Pour hot brine over olives in jars and cork tightly. Wash olives in clean cold water and dry in soft towel before serving.

ONIONS

■ Milk is good when frying onions. Soak sliced onions for 15 minutes in milk first, they will then fry to delicious brown with a new flavour.
■ Peel onions without tears. Plunge them into boiling water first.

Onion Flakes

White onions are preferable. Slice onions and cut across slices several times. Boil for 2 to 3 minutes to kill bacteria. Cool in cold water. Roughly dry with old towel or clean rag. Put in slow oven or warmer to dry until crisp. Put in jar or plastic bag when completely cold and dry. The flakes can be used to flavour stews or soups. Soak in boiling water for a few minutes and put in vinegar, they spice up a salad. Once dried, the flakes can be crushed as finely as required.

OVEN
Cleaning Tips

■ Save on oven cleaning by lining the bottom of the oven with a sheet of thick aluminium foil cut to fit. This catches all grease and is easily removed and replaced when dirty.

■ Grease will be easier to remove from ovens after cooking if you put a few drops of ammonia in a dish and place in oven. Or sprinkle crumpled newspaper with ammonia and place in oven.

■ To remove boiled-over syrup on enamel oven shelf, use Hi-Speed Frypan and Cookware Cleaner. Removes all stubborn stains and baked-on grease.

■ Burnt-in stains are harder to remove. Scrape off as much as possible with a blunt knife, wipe over with cold water. Clean stove with Mr. Muscle, spray and leave overnight.

■ To prevent your stove or washing machine soiling, wax first.

■ Another good oven cleaner is cloudy ammonia which will dissolve burnt-on dirt. Wipe out the oven thoroughly afterwards.

PAINT BRUSHES

Hard paint brushes will soften after an hour if placed in hot vinegar.

PAINTED WOOD
Spruce Up Painted Wood

■ For dirty painted wood in kitchen, wash with a weak solution of sugar soap bought at hardware store. Wear rubber gloves.

■ Want to clean painted woodwork? Dissolve 2 tablespoons borax in boiling water and add to a bowl of lukewarm soapsuds. Wash woodwork with a soft cloth soaked in this solution, rinse, dry thoroughly. To remove marks like smudges, finger marks or greasy stains, add a little paraffin to the soapy lather and use as above.

■ Prevent yellowing of newly painted white cupboards in your kitchen. Take a piece of cotton cloth, like an old knitted vest, rinse in lukewarm soapy water. Wring out then sprinkle well with solution of equal parts kerosene and methylated spirits. Wipe doors once a week.

■ Wipe white kitchen cupboards once a week with bleach, using a soft cloth. Finish with another dry cloth.

PAINTING

■ Two thin coats of paint are much better than one thick one.

PANTYHOSE

To make new pantyhose last longer, wet them thoroughly, wring out gently, place in a plastic bag and toss into the freezer. Once frozen, thaw in sink or tub and then hang to dry.

PARSLEY
Dried Parsley

■ To dry and keep parsley for winter use, tie into bunches and boil for 5 minutes in slightly salted water. Drain from the water on to a sieve. Dry very quickly and put into jars. When required for use, soak parsley in warm water for a few minutes.

■ Keep the colour and flavour of parsley. Dry quickly in a warm oven preheated to 120°C.

Long Life for Fresh Parsley

Parsley stored unwashed in a tightly sealed jar will stay fresh longer.

Keep Those Parsley Stalks

Use parsley stalks to flavour soups and stews.

PASSIONFRUIT
Saving Passionfruit Pulp

Avoid cooking with iron, galvanised iron, copper or brass utensils. Passionfruit should be handled only with aluminium, unchipped enamel or stainless steel equipment. Select fully ripe fruit, cut in half and scoop out pulp. Add from 110 g to 225 g sugar to each 600 ml of pulp. Add preservative in the form of 4 grains of potassium metabisulphite per 600 ml of pulp. Dissolve the required amounts of preservative, which your chemist will obtain and weigh out for you, in a little water and stir into the pulp. Heat rapidly in an uncovered saucepan, stirring constantly to avoid scorching, to a temperature of 77°C. Pour at once into hot sterile bottles. Fill to overflowing and seal immediately with sterile seals. Turn bottles upside down away from draughts and store in a cool, dark place. Or pour into sterilised jars, screw on plastic or glass lids and store in fridge. The passionfruit will last 6–9 months.

Quick and Easy Pulp Preservation

This really simple method involves putting passionfruit pulp in ice cube trays and freezing. When frozen, take from trays and place in plastic bags. Secure tops of bags, keep in fridge.

Store Fruit in the Fridge

Passionfruit can be placed straight from the vine into the freezer. There is even no need for freezer bags. Passionfruit will keep this way for at least 12 months and taste just as if freshly picked.

PASTRY

■ For **crisper, tastier pastry**, add a tablespoon of powdered milk to the flour. Mix with ice cold water to which a squeeze of lemon juice has been added.

■ For a really crisp biscuit pastry, add 1 teaspoon white vinegar to the water used when making pies or tarts.

■ **Sweet pastry** will be light and lovely if you use icing sugar instead of ordinary sugar.

■ Custard powder is also good added to sweet pastry, as it makes it beautifully crisp and brown when cooked. Add a dessertspoonful to the flour and salt.

■ Add a large tablespoon of coconut to the flour and sugar before adding shortening when making **short pastry** for apple pies, etc. Makes a delicious and different pastry.

■ Sprinkle custard powder on the board before rolling out pastry to give an attractive brown finish.

■ Use a piece of plastic over the pastry board when rolling out scone dough, pastry or biscuits. You'll find it's much easier to clean than the pastry board.

■ Try this good **egg substitute** when glazing pastry: boil 1 tablespoon brown sugar in 2 tablespoons milk. Cool and brush over pastry before baking.

■ To make a light pastry glaze, dissolve 1 teaspoon castor sugar in 2 teaspoons hot water. Let cool and use for sweet pastry. To make a pale **brown glaze** use beaten egg, and to give a rich brown colour use beaten egg yolk only. Equal quantities of beaten egg and cold water produce a good economical glaze. Apply in all cases with a fine pastry brush and work lightly but thoroughly over surfaces of pastry.

■ If your pastry is browning too quickly in the oven, cover it with foil.

Filo Pastry Hints

If using frozen filo pastry, leave in its plastic cover until completely thawed. Do not take out of plastic until ready to use. When removing pastry from pack, have bundle flattened out and remove gently, then brush melted butter between each layer of pastry until you have required amount. Always cover with wet tea towel as soon as you use, which stops it drying and breaking. Spread on apple mixture, diced apple, brown sugar, cinnamon, sultanas and nutmeg. Roll or fold up and cook.

PATENT LEATHER

Prevent patent leather becoming dry and cracking. Every month, rub with warmed petroleum jelly. Polish with soft cloth.

PATHS

■ Remove rust marks and black tyre paint from concrete with brake fluid. Pour on and scrub marks, hose off. Or, try hydrochloric acid diluted one to 10 parts water. Please note, be careful using this. Wear rubber gloves as this acid burns the skin.

■ Oil stains on concrete floors or paths can be removed by washing with paraffin or petrol. Rinse off with caustic soda solution. Once stains have been treated, remove all traces of caustic soda by swilling floor thoroughly with clean water.

■ To remove oil stains from the driveway, shake sand over to absorb the oil, then wash concrete with detergent.

■ Any candle grease on unpainted cement? Take a hot iron out to the cement. Press iron over brown paper on the candle grease. Keep moving brown paper to a fresh spot until all grease has melted into paper. Reheat iron if necessary. Now dissolve some powdered borax in hot water — 5 tablespoons to 5 litres — and scrub the spots with a strong nail brush or scrubbing brush. Cement will come up white and new looking.

■ To remove moss from a path, mix equal parts of draught vinegar and methylated spirits. Apply with a scrubbing brush. Scrub well. Leave for 15 minutes, then scrub surface again with mixture. Leave another 15 minutes, hose off and sweep with a broom. If heavily coated with moss and slime, repeat again.

■ For slippery concrete steps, paint with clear paving paint, then sieve fine sand over before paint dries.

PAVLOVA
Why That Pav is Weeping

Pavlova leaks syrup during cooking when the sugar is not properly dissolved. In some recipes, castor sugar is used for quick dissolving; for others granulated sugar gives a firmer result. It is important, when beating sugar into egg whites, to make sure all the sugar is dissolved, otherwise the undissolved sugar will melt during cooking and give a 'weepy' sticky pavlova. To test if sugar is dissolved, rub a little of the mixture between two fingers. Any undissolved sugar crystals can be quickly detected. Cornflour in a recipe also prevents 'weeping'.

■ See recipes under *Cooking*.

PEANUT BUTTER

To make your own peanut butter, place 225 g shelled, roasted or salted peanuts, 2 tablespoons peanut oil and (if nuts are unsalted) ¾ teaspoon salt in blender. Turn on to low speed until nuts are coarsely chopped. If a crunchy style is what you fancy, blend at high speed for ½ a minute. For a creamy style, blend on high speed for 2 minutes. Mixture will become firm on standing. Makes about 1 cup.

PEANUTS
To Cook Raw Peanuts

■ Roasted in shells. Heat oven to 200°C and place nuts in shells on tray one layer thick. Cook for 12 to 15 minutes, according to taste.

■ Salted peanuts. Place shelled nuts on tray and cook at 200°C for 7 to 10 minutes turning occasionally, allow to cool enough to handle and rub to remove skins. Sprinkle with salt.

■ Beer nuts. Place 1 tablespoon peanut oil in frying pan and heat to 200°C. Add 2 cups peanuts and 1 tablespoon salt. Cook for 15 minutes, stirring occasionally.

■ Devilled nuts. As for Beer nuts but add 2 teaspoons curry powder.

PEARLS
How to Clean Cultured Pearls

■ Place pearls in plastic bag with a handful of dry raw rice. Shake bag gently. The smooth rice will polish the pearls and help bring back their lustre.

■ Ordinary bran is another friend to cultured pearls. Place bran in ovenproof dish or saucepan and heat, stirring occasionally. Remove from heat. Place pearls in hot bran, cover and leave until cold. Remove pearls and wipe with clean towel. Should be as good as new.

PERSPEX
Goodbye Perspex Scratches

Perspex is cellulose. The dissolver of cellulose is lacquer thinner, also known as nail polish remover. Apply a small quantity to a clean pad, and apply to scratches with quick, light strokes always in the one direction. Should remove most of them. Do not, at any stage, allow the pad to sit on top of the perspex because it is a dissolver. If the scratches are very deep, the following mixture gives excellent results. Mix a level teaspoon of either Silvo or Brasso with a level teaspoon of white toothpaste. Apply on a clean pad rubbing in a backward and forward movement. This cuts and polishes the scratches out. Finish off with a clean linen cloth.

PEWTER

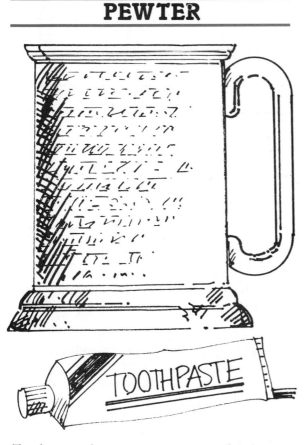

To clean and restore pewter, mix finely powdered whiting with a little oil and apply to pewter with a soft cloth. Rub in well, then polish with a clean cloth, giving a final rub with a chamois leather. Ordinary toothpaste is also effective in cleaning pewter. Apply with a soft cloth and leave about 4 minutes. Then polish and remove toothpaste with polishing cloth. Always clean in the one direction, with the grain of the pewter. Rinse articles in warm water after cleaning, as pewter tends to absorb dirty soapy marks otherwise. Use a soft cloth to wipe at this point. Then dry with a soft clean towel.

PHOTOGRAPHS

Photographs can be cleaned by rubbing gently with cottonwool dipped in methylated spirits.

Unstick Those Snaps

To treat colour photos stuck together due to heat, simply soak in lukewarm water until they separate. This could take up to 6 hours but they will simply drift apart. Do not mop or wipe dry, just dab them dry. Do not use this method for hand-coloured photographs.

Replace Mildewed Photo Backings

If picture backing is damp or mildewed, it is often better to replace it completely. Small pieces of rubber glued to the back of a picture frame stop paper on the back wearing away.

Prevent Mildewed Photos

Keep pictures slightly away from wall to allow the air to circulate and help prevent backs from becoming damp and mildewed. Four drawing pins pressed into the back corners of the frame would also keep the picture backing from wearing through contact with the wall.

No Dirt Inside Picture Frames

Seal backs of pictures or photographs with a sheet of plywood about 3 mm thick. Attach this backing to frame with tiny little tacks. Stops dirt from forming on inside of glass.

PIANOS

Hang a bag of mothballs inside your piano to prevent mustiness in damp weather and to deter moths and silverfish.

PICKLES

■ To remove the salty taste from choko pickles, peel and cut up two or three potatoes in small chunks, place with pickles in saucepan and simmer slowly for ½ an hour or more. The potatoes will absorb all the salt.

■ Add two or three lumps of sugar to the vinegar when making pickles and rinse the jars well with vinegar. This is one way to prevent fermentation.

PIKELETS

■ See recipes under *Cooking*.

PLAY DOUGH

Play Dough 1

1 cup each plain flour and water
½ cup salt
1 tablespoon baby oil
2 tablespoons cream of tartar
food colouring
Mix together and boil until thickened.
Makes one margarine tub full.

Play Dough 2

2 cups bicarb soda
1 cup cornflour
1 ¼ cups cold water
Stir together bicarb soda and cornflour in a saucepan. Add water and cook over medium heat, stirring constantly. When mixture is consistency of moist mashed potatoes, turn out onto a plate and cover with a damp cloth. When cool enough to handle, knead like dough, then shape as desired. Can be stored in a tightly sealed plastic bag in the refrigerator for later use. Colour can be added as the clay is being made, or pieces can be painted after they have been allowed to dry. Coat objects with clear varnish or shellac for a protective finish.

PLAYING CARDS

■ See *Cards*.

POLISHING CLOTH

A good polishing cloth for mirrors can be made from flannelette. Rinse the cloth in water, adding a tablespoon of turpentine. Gives a lasting polish.

POPCORN

■ See recipes under *Cooking*.

PORK

Crisp Crackling

■ Make rind of pork crisp and crackly by rubbing over with olive oil and salt before cooking.

■ Have butcher score the pork, or do it yourself with a sharp knife, making 6 mm parallel cuts. Rub well with peanut or vegetable oil and sprinkle top with salt, rubbing lightly into score cuts. Put enough oil on bottom of baking dish to prevent pork sticking. Put in a hot oven 230°C for first 20 minutes, then turn oven down to 180°C. Never baste or turn pork over, always have crackling uppermost. Allow 30 to 40 minutes per 500 g, or bake until crackling is a delicious crisp brown.

PORRIDGE

Malted milk powder sprinkled on porridge adds flavour and is very nourishing.

POTATOES

Keep Potatoes White

■ Put a tablespoonful white vinegar in the water before boiling or steaming. This is sufficient for 2 to 3 people; if cooking larger amounts, use more vinegar.

■ To prevent potatoes discolouring while boiling, add a few drops of lemon juice to the water.

Farewell Watery, Mushy Spuds

■ If potatoes are watery when cooking, add 1 teaspoon full cream powdered milk to every cupful potatoes. Dries up moisture and gives good flavour.

■ If potatoes are mushy, beat in an egg, whipping until potatoes thicken.

Brilliant Baked Potatoes

■ Baked potatoes are delicious if pre-boiled in consomme made with a stock cube.

■ For crusty baked potatoes, first boil them for about 5 minutes, roll in seasoned flour then bake as usual with the roast.

Crisp Chips

■ Soak thinly sliced potatoes for chips in iced water for 30 minutes before cooking. Dry thoroughly. This prevents them becoming soggy.

■ Chips brown more quickly if a pinch of salt is added to the fat.

Copha Chips

Peel 450 g potatoes and cut into chips. Place in a bowl of cold water to remove excess starch. Heat copha in deep frying pan over low heat. The pan should be half full of melted copha. Drain water from chips and dry well in clean tea towel. When copha has reached 188°C place dried chips in a frying basket and lower slowly in the hot copha. Deep fry for 5 minutes, remove from pan and allow copha to reheat. Lower chips back into hot copha and fry until golden brown. Drain chips well on kitchen paper, sprinkle with a little salt and serve immediately. Copha chips taste delicious as they are free from any greasy flavour.

Mashed Potatoes

■ Warm the butter and milk before adding to potatoes to keep them light, fluffy and creamy.

■ When mashing potatoes, add a teaspoon of baking powder with the milk. Potatoes will rise and be fluffier.

■ No butter is needed in mashed potatoes if you use evaporated milk. They taste better and are creamier.

■ When serving mashed potatoes with cold meats, mix a little grated cheese through after mashing. Gives a special flavour.

■ When serving mashed potatoes with pork or veal, add a little orange juice and grated rind for delicious flavour.

■ To make potatoes go further, add 1 cup of well cooked rice and mash together with a little butter and chopped parsley.

■ See recipes under *Cooking*.

POT-POURRI
Three Lovely Mixtures

■ Mix together 50 g dried lavender flowers, 50 g powdered orris root, 25 g ground rosemary, 5 drops oil of rose. Store 6 weeks in closed, dark glass jar, then make into individual pot-pourris.

■ In dry weather gather any fragrant flower petals, leaves or herbs you can find. Spread them on sheets of paper and allow to dry in a warm atmosphere, but out of direct sunlight, for two to three weeks, until they are crisp to touch. To each cupful of dried mixture, add 1 teaspoon each of common salt, cloves, cinnamon, allspice and nutmeg, all ground, plus two teaspoons orris root from chemist. Mix all the ingredients well, cover pot-pourri and leave a few days to mature. The mixture may need crushing before filling into sachets.

■ Pick about three dozen roses and spread the petals out on paper. Leave them to dry indoors, away from strong sunlight. Pick any other strongly perfumed flowers and dry separately. Turn the rose petals frequently and leave until almost as dry as paper. Put dried rose petals into a container including a small handful of common salt to every handful of petals. Cover and leave for 5 days. Gather the following ingredients: 110 g powdered orris root, 30 g coriander seed, 30 g grated nutmeg, 30 g whole cloves, 2 to 3 sticks cinnamon, 15 g lavender oil. After five days, add the other dried flowers to the rose petals. Mix the oil with some of the orris root, add the rest of the spices, etc, then add to the dried flowers. Stir well, cover and leave for 3 to 4 weeks, stirring occasionally. If the mixture is too moist, add more orris, if too dry, add more salt. Keep pot-pourri in a pottery or glass jar or bowl, or in sachets.

POULTRY
Stuffings and Seasonings

■ Cut up a cooking apple, half an onion and a rasher of bacon, and put inside before roasting for a quick and tasty stuffing.

■ Season a chicken with 2 cups soft breadcrumbs, ½ cup chopped nuts, 1 egg, 1 dessertspoon butter, ½ teaspoon lemon juice, salt and pepper.

■ Mix a teaspoon of coconut with the breadcrumbs. This keeps your bird moist and gives a nice richness to breadcrumbs. And for meat stuffing, orange rind or a mushroom stock cube gives an interesting flavour.

■ When cooking poultry add a teaspoon ground ginger to the sage and onion stuffing. Delicious.

■ Add ½ teaspoon baking powder to the dry ingredients for poultry seasoning and it will never be soggy.

Golden Baked Chicken

■ Rub chickens with oil before baking to make a golden shiny skin.

■ To prevent chicken sticking to pan when baking, place 1 or 2 slices bread between chicken and greased baking dish. A little vinegar in the pan with the dripping has the same effect. Does not affect the flavour. Also works well with fried fish.

■ See recipes under *Cooking*.

PUMPKIN
Reasons for Non-Productive Vines

Pumpkins turn yellow and fall off the vine for two main reasons: uneven or insufficient water supply or lack of pollination. Give pumpkins setting fruit a plentiful, steady supply of water. If the fallen gourds are very small, failure to pollinate is the reason. Take pollen from the male flowers with a fingertip or small brush and transfer to the female flowers, those with tiny pumpkins beneath them. Then the fruit should develop. If both these remedies fail, there is probably some deficiency of the soil which could lack nitrogen. Use a complete plant food.

Pumpkins Fresh as Daisies

■ After cutting from the vine, cut pumpkin into segments, peel and remove all trace of seeds and pulp. Then store in plastic bags, tightly closed with twisters, in the fridge, not freezing compartment. Stays fresh for up to 3 weeks.

■ After cutting and removing all seeds and soft area around the seeds, put 1 cup plain flour in a plastic bag. Place pieces of pumpkin in bag and shake well, making sure all cut surfaces are covered with the flour. Will keep in the vegetable section of your fridge for many weeks. Flour can be washed off prior to cooking. This method is very good providing all the centre is well scraped out of a large pumpkin. Use a spoon, and make sure you are on the firm pumpkin before flouring.

PUTTY

To make putty for filling wide cracks in wood or fibro mix whiting and linseed oil to the consistency of dough in an ice cream container. Place in an airtight container. If the putty becomes too dry, add more linseed oil. If putty is too thin, just add a little more whiting.

QUARRY TILES

To remove cooking grease stains from quarry tiles use a cloth wet with about 1 teaspoon cloudy ammonia. Rub over greasy stains. Repeat if required.

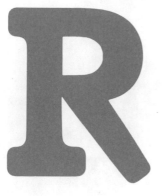

RECORDS
Buckled Records

Put them between two sheets of glass and place in sun on a flat surface. About an hour later take inside house, still between the glass. Allow them to cool to room temperature, remove glass and records will be as good as new. If badly buckled, place a weight on the glass for extra flatness.

Scratched Records

Wipe all dust off the record, making sure the grooves are clean. Take 1 tablespoon olive oil and soak clean cloth or hankie with it. Rub record with oiled cloth. Let record dry, not allowing it to touch anything. About a week should be long enough. When dry, record is OK to use. Rub scratches with a black felt marker available from paper shops. Play record with bad scratches and apply felt marker once again.

Recycle Your Records

Cover old, scratched records with aluminium foil and use as cake plates. Makes a very good base.

REFRIGERATORS

■ **Deodorise** inside of fridge by washing with a teaspoon of dry mustard in soapy water. Vanilla in warm water is also good.

■ **Polish** the refrigerator and other enamelled appliances with car polish.

■ To remove **mould** from around your fridge door, dip an old toothbrush in methylated spirits and scrub rubber. Wipe down, rinse brush thoroughly and brush again with warm suds. Wipe with clean wet cloth and dry. Could need going over twice with methylated spirits and clean brush if in bad condition. Rubber comes up very clean.

■ For mould on rubber fridge door seal, use 1 tablespoon household bleach in half cup lukewarm water. Dip a toothbrush in solution, rub off mould then wash rubber with clean lukewarm water and dry. The bleach kills the mould spores. If very stubborn, neat bleach can be used but be sure to wash well afterwards.

REGISTRATION STICKERS

Expired registration stickers or decals are easily removed from car windscreens (no need for that tiresome scraping). Just rub sticker firmly with a wad of cottonwool well soaked in nail polish remover. Sticker will gradually dissolve. Clean windscreen with methylated spirits and apply new sticker as directed.

RELISH

■ See recipes under *Cooking*.

RHUBARB

A spoonful of marmalade added when cooking rhubarb improves the flavour.

RICE
Tips for Cooking Rice

■ To make three cups of rice, add 1 cup uncooked, unwashed rice to 8 cups rapidly boiling water with 1 level dessertspoon salt added. Boil rapidly for precisely 15 minutes with the lid off the saucepan. Then tip all remaining water with the cooked rice immediately into a colander or sieve. Do not rinse or stir, simply shake colander and serve at once.

■ Squeeze lemon juice on rice when boiling to whiten and separate the grains.

■ A teaspoon of butter or margarine added when boiling rice prevents the grains sticking together.

■ Rice will be snow-white and fluffy with each grain separated if you add a flat teaspoon of bicarbonate of soda to the water when it reaches boiling point.

■ To keep rice hot for a few minutes before serving, tip back into saucepan after shaking well in colander.

RISSOLES AND MEATBALLS
Handy Hints

■ Add one teaspoon baking powder to 500 g minced steak when making rissoles. Makes them rise and keeps them light.

■ To bind rissoles, one teaspoon gelatine dissolved in half a cup of water takes the place of an egg. Roll in breadcrumbs and leave until firm before frying.

■ When making rissoles or cutlets using breadcrumbs, bind crumbs with custard powder in the milk instead of eggs. Makes the cutlets a golden brown.

■ Dip rissoles in cold water before rolling them in flour. This prevents them from cracking.

■ Use an ice-cream scoop when making meatballs. Saves times and the meatballs are all the same size.

ROASTS

■ When roasting a joint, place two lumps of sugar in pan. This helps make gravy brown.

■ See recipes under *Cooking*.

ROLLING PINS

Need a rolling pin? Fill a bottle with iced water. Makes a marvellous roller.

ROSES
Dried Roses — How To Do It

■ Pick roses at their best. They must be dry, with no dew or rain clinging. Cut stems to 2 cm from bloom and insert a piece of florist wire about 5 cm long into base. Use an ice cream container or similar dish and sprinkle powdered borax in the bottom. Place roses in, face up. Cover gently with more borax. They must be completely covered. Leave in a dry place for 3 weeks then carefully take out using a soft brush to remove borax. Longer wires can be added to the short ones and these stems rolled in florist tape. Arrange flowers in suitable vase, or a large, upturned jar. Keep away from sunlight. They keep well in airtight container.

■ Drying in borax is ideal, giving a more natural look and a truer colour than other methods. Dark colours tend to darken a little, pale ones become a little paler, white dries perfectly.

RUGS
Whiten Your Flokati Rug

Soak rug in very lukewarm water with Bio-Ad. Directions on packet. If rug is very yellow, you can add a little extra powder. Also dissolve a couple of tablespoons borax in the water. Soak rug overnight. Next morning rub rug well or put in washing machine in the water in which it soaked overnight. Rinse well adding a little washing blue to the last rinse. Rug should then be fresh and white again.

Slipping Mats

■ Strips of foam or rubber rings can be stitched to the back of bathroom mats to stop slipping. Ideal rings are those in Vacola bottling outfits, available at most hardware stores.

■ Buy thin foam rubber. Cut to the same size as mats and sew to the back by machine. Will stand up to machine washings.

SANDFLIES

Stop the itch of sandfly bites almost immediately by applying equal quantities of cold tea and methylated spirits.

SAUCEPANS
Cleaning a Burnt Saucepan

■ Cover bottom of saucepan with 6 mm vinegar and 1 tablespoon cooking salt. Leave overnight. Pour liquid away, then scour pan.

■ Badly burnt saucepans can be cleaned by gently heating a little olive oil in them. Allow to stand an hour, pour off oil and clean in usual way.

■ Cover base of saucepan with cold water and add a small chopped onion. Boil for about 10 minutes. Food will clean off quickly and easily. If not the first time, repeat using same onion and fresh water.

■ Put a dessertspoon cooking salt and carbsoda in pan, fill with hot water and leave stand for a couple of days. Most burnt matter will scrape off, use scourer if necessary.

■ See also **Aluminium, Cast-iron Cookware.**

SCENT SACHET

Create a sweet-smelling scent sachet. It's easy. Add a few drops of your favourite perfume to a few teaspoons of oatmeal. After mixing well, put into a tiny satin bag and tie with matching ribbon. A nice idea for fetes.

SCISSORS

Sharpen scissors by cutting through a piece of coarse sandpaper several times. This also works wonders with machine needles. Sew a few stitches through sandpaper with an unthreaded needle.

SCONES
Tips for Cooking Scones

■ Instead of rubbing butter into scone or sponge dough, melt it in the milk or water. Scones and cakes will be fluffier.

■ Use hot milk in scone mixture instead of cold. Scones will rise better and be much lighter.

■ Add one junket tablet, plain, not flavoured, to one cup of milk when making scones. This gives the thick milk which makes the best dough.

■ Sweet scones will be as light and fluffy as plain ones if you dissolve the sugar in the liquid used for mixing instead of adding it to the flour.

■ Tomato juice instead of milk in scones gives them a savoury taste. They're delicious served hot with butter and cheese.

■ Glaze cakes, scones, pastry by brushing with well mixed brown sugar and milk, instead of egg white.

■ For a sweet brown crust on scones, sift a little icing sugar over them before baking.

■ Freshen stale scones by wrapping in foil and leaving in moderate oven for 20 minutes.

■ Turn heavy, poorly risen scones into fried tea cakes. Split scones in half. Dip in beaten egg mixed with a little milk. Fry in plenty of butter until crisp and golden. Serve piping hot, smothered with castor sugar and cinnamon.

SCREWTOP JARS

When a screwtop jar refuses to open, hold a piece of coarse sandpaper around the lid to give a firm grip. If still stuck, turn jar upside down and hold the lid only in hot water. Will turn easily in a few seconds.

SEAGRASS

Clean seagrass chairs with a good soap powder in hot water with a little ammonia added. Brush seagrass with this solution, then hose chair and leave in sun to dry.

SEASONINGS
Substitute Seasoning

■ Instead of making seasoning for chicken, cut up a cooking apple, half an onion and a rasher of bacon and put inside before roasting.

Taste Treat

■ Improve the flavour of sage and onion seasoning. Add a large cooking apple, peeled and chopped.

SEAT BELTS
To Clean Seat Belts

Protect car seats with coverings, squeeze Blue Clinic hair shampoo liberally over seat belts. Wear gloves. Rub gently up and down with palms of hands for several moments until shampoo saturates belts and loosens dirt. Move to next belt and repeat. Take a plastic bowl of warm water and repeat rinsing until water is clear. Will need a helper to hold the bowl of water while rinsing belts. Rub dry with old towel. Belts will be really clean and have a very pleasant smell.

SEAWEED
Scrumptious Seaweed Balls

seaweed
salt
oatmeal
fat

After washing seaweed in clean water with a handful of added salt, place in large saucepan with just sufficient water to cover base. Cover with a piece of cloth or old clean teatowel. Steam the weed for at least 2 hours. Remove cloth and wring out surplus moisture, then replace cloth. Allow to cool, then mince or chop finely. Finally form into round balls, coat with oatmeal and fry in bacon fat or fat from beef or steak. Do not allow seaweed to become too soggy and wet while cooking, keep more on the dry side, otherwise will be difficult to mince.

SEEDS
Simple Seed Boxes

■ Empty matchboxes make good containers for seeds.
■ Cardboard egg containers make good planters for seeds.
■ An old suitcase makes an ideal seed box. Fill with soil, plant seeds. At night, the lid can be shut to keep frost and pests away.
■ Foil line shallow cardboard boxes or cartons with aluminium foil for growing seedlings. They'll be ready later for lifting out and transplanting.

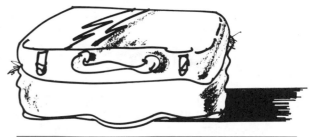

Scat, Cat!

Keep cats away from seedlings by putting small bottles containing ammonia in the soil, buried up to the necks, among the plants.

Economy Tip

Are you a garden lover? Buy a packet of seeds instead of seedlings. You will find 12 seedlings cost more than 100 seeds.

SEWING
Making it easy

When gathering a long piece of material by hand, thread needle and leave cotton on the reel. Presto, there's no long thread to annoy you and the thread is never too short.

Keep loose needles in a cork to prevent them rusting and pricking your finger when searching in a drawer.

SHAMPOO

To make your own shampoo you need a cake of toilet soap. Put it in a saucepan, pour on 600 ml of boiling water and simmer until soap dissolves. When cool, pour into a wide mouthed jar, adding, if you like, a little bay rum or eau-de-cologne. When cold, soap mixture will form a jelly that can be mixed as required with a little hot water and rubbed into scalp like an ordinary shampoo.

SHEEPSKIN
Remove Sheepskin Smell

To remove natural sheepskin odour, wash first in warm soapy water. Do not use a detergent. Then rinse twice in warm water. The second rinse takes care of the odour. For a lamb-size skin, use 1 teaspoon eucalyptus or oil of rosemary in the second rinse. For a full-grown skin, you need 1 tablespoon.

Give sheepskin slippers an occasional sponge with warm water containing a teaspoon of lavender oil. This keeps skin fragrant.

slippers

SHEEP TONGUES
To Peel Sheep Tongues

■ When putting tongues on to cook, add a little bicarbonate of soda to the cold water. Cook thoroughly and peel immediately.
■ Add a tablespoon of vinegar to the water and you'll find the skin will come off easily.

SHELLS
Cleaning Oyster Shells

Soak fresh, new shells in a dish of boiling water with some detergent and a cap of Milton, a bacterial solution used for sterilising baby bottles. Let stand overnight. Next day scrub thoroughly. Use an extra hard tooth brush bought for that purpose. Get into all crevices and clean off all particles of flesh, that's a must. Rinse and place in saucepan covered with water and another cap of Milton. Boil for about half hour, let cool, drain off water. Place each shell up-ended on a tray and dry off thoroughly, another must! Best placed in sun as they dry out more quickly. No need to rinse first. Only boil the shells when you first get them. After that, soak overnight, then clean and dry. Store in 4 litre ice cream container.

Polishing Shells

Wash thoroughly in warm soapy water until shell is clean. When dry, coat with clear gloss varnish, using two or three coatings. Clam shells are treated in the Pacific Islands by brushing the outer shells with a solution of equal parts of muriatic acid (spirits of salts) and water. Take care to protect hands with rubber gloves as this solution is very strong. Wash off the solution at intervals to inspect the cleaning process. Do not allow solution to reach or damage the inner surface of the shell.

To polish the internal shell surface, use Brasso metal polish. Make a small pad of clean rag and firmly rub shell with plenty of polish. Clean off with clean polishing rag. The white shell will soon take on a high polish.

SHOE POLISH

Shoe polish which has hardened can be softened. Add a few drops of olive oil, turpentine or kerosene and put tin in a warm oven for a few minutes.

SHOES AND BOOTS

■ Before cleaning **sandshoes**, dampen them with milk. Gives a very white effect and keeps them white much longer.

■ If new white **tennis shoes** are sprayed with starch before wearing and after each cleaning, they will stay white longer.

■ To clean **sandshoes** or **bowling shoes**, use a piece of foam plastic to apply white cleaner. Doesn't splash like a toothbrush.

■ **Stains on white or bone** shoes can often be removed by rubbing with a soft pencil eraser.

■ Rub Sard Wonder soap on a damp rag and gently but firmly rub over white shoes until trouble spots disappear. Rinse soap off completely with clean wet rag, then wipe with dry rag to absorb as much dampness as possible. Allow to finish drying in the shade. Handbags may also be cleaned like this.

■ To remove scuff marks on boots, buy Nugget Scuff Stuff liquid shoe polish. This has a sponge applicator on top and comes in black, brown or tan. Directions on the pack. Good for covering all scuff and scratch marks on leather boots or shoes. Texta felt pens in colour of the leather can also be used to cover up marks and scratches.

■ Salt and water stains can be removed from boots or heavy shoes with vinegar or rubbing alcohol. Wipe over the stained area only, then polish. Remove accumulated salt stains by wiping leather with a flannel cloth dipped in milk. Then rub saddle soap into the leather and wipe away residue.

■ To clean Ugg boots, first spray them with a pre-wash solution. Leave for specified time. Make a small, slightly stronger solution of wool shampoo. Scrub well with a stiff scrubbing brush until dirt is removed. Do not over-wet, just dip brush into shampoo. May take longer scrubbing if boots have been soiled with oil or grease. Hang on line to dry. Then spray with Selley's Waterproofing, two or three times.

■ The only way to keep Ugg boots worn outside in good condition is to change their colour. Before wearing, use Meltonian Colour Change to dye and waterproof. Two bottles are enough for one pair. When boots need cleaning just touch-up.

■ To clean sheepskin linings in boots, sprinkle liberally with powdered starch. Leave overnight, then brush well outdoors.

Adios, Shoe Odours

■ Sprinkle inside shoes with Johnson's Vemo deodorant powder. Allow to stand overnight or for a day or two. If necessary, repeat process.

■ Bicarbonate of soda can be very effective. Sprinkle thickly into the shoes, making sure the powder reaches the very tips, then leave with powder inside for several days. Shake out and air shoes. All odour will have gone.

■ Camphor is effective in keeping shoe cupboards and shoes stored in them really fresh.

Slippery Soles

Use a thin layer of Jumbo Soling Compound or Selley's Spreadsole. Use as directed on packs for a long-lasting rough surface for your soles.

Storing Shoes

Put suede, leather and plastic shoes in plastic bags with epsom salts. Shoes stored this way for a long time show no trace of mould or mildew. This method is also suitable for clothing.

Lazy Daisy Slippers

If toes of velvet or felt slippers become worn, embroider closely with lazy daisy flowers.

SHOWERS
To Clean Plastic Shower Curtains

Rub soiled side while wet with powdered borax. Soapy film will simply lift off.

SILVER
Cleaning Stained Silver

Put 57 g washing soda into 600 ml water in an enamelled pan, add a few milk bottle tops or any scraps of aluminium. Boil the silver articles in this until stains have gone. Never use metal polish on silver. Clean with plate powder moistened with methylated spirit or water. For pewter, clean with whiting moistened with linseed oil. Wash off in soap and water, rinse and polish with a dry cloth.

Tarnished Silver Plate

■ Boil in an aluminium saucepan with enough water to cover the articles. Add one teaspoon cream of tartar to the water and boil for 10 minutes. Wash, then polish the silver with a good silver polishing cloth.

■ Silverware will shine if polished with a paste of starch and methylated spirits (moisten about 1 teaspoon of starch with the spirits). Allow to dry on silver, then rub off.

Silver Polish

Use a plate powder like Goddards. Put equal parts cold water, plate powder, cloudy ammonia and methylated spirits in a screw top jar. Shake well before using.

Silver Polishing Cloths

■ Mix one teaspoon silver powder cleaner with one tablespoon methylated spirits in one cup cold water. Cut a soft cloth, flannelette is good, about 46 cm square. Soak this in the mixture, do not squeeze out, then hang on line to dry. Store in plastic bag. Use to rub up forks and spoons or any silver. Cloth will last for years.

■ Cut pieces of flannelette or towelling into 30 cm squares and soak in this mixture: 1 tablespoon each Goddards plate powder and cloudy ammonia and 600 ml water. This is sufficient for 4 cloths and should last for 6 months or longer. Soak cloths in mixture until all is absorbed, do not squeeze out, hang to dry. Ready to use when dry.

■ Mix 1 cup each whiting and ammonia and 2 cups water. Soak flannel or similar fabric cut in squares for 30 minutes, wring out and allow to dry thoroughly. Will keep silver shining and not cause any damage. Must be very dry before use.

Souvenir Spoons

To prevent metals from tarnishing when displaying or storing, rub with petroleum jelly after cleaning.

Shining Stored Silver

Prevent silverware which is stored from tarnishing by wrapping in aluminium foil.

SILVERFISH
Stop These Pests

■ Spirits of turpentine is a sure preventative against moths and silverfish. Simply dropping a little in the bottom of drawers, chests and cupboards will render garments secure from pests during the summer months. Note: spirits of turpentine, oil of turpentine or pure turpentine are one and the same. Mineral turpentine is a completely different product.

■ Use unwrapped cakes of soap, plus a few whole cloves and you will never be troubled with destructive silverfish. Just place among clothes or in the pocket of a fur coat.

■ Keep silverfish out of dark cupboards by lining shelves with newspaper.

■ Keep silverfish and moths away from drawers. Wipe over the wood with eucalyptus.

■ Use epsom salts for good results. Sprinkle where silverfish are seen, renewing every four months or when salts begin to get powdery. For drawers, kitchen cupboards, wardrobes, bookcases and so forth.

■ Camphor blocks banish silverfish just as well as naphthalene flakes.

■ Mineral turps sprayed from an atomiser on the back of mats after cleaning will keep away fleas and silverfish.

SINKS
Smelly Sink?

A few coffee grounds poured down the sink will prove a good sweetener. Coffee grounds are excellent smell-removers. Apart from deodorising sinks, they are also good for removing burnt and unsavoury smells. Put a tablespoon or two of grounds into a pan and burn on top of the stove to remove such strong kitchen smells as onions and fish. Or sprinkle a few tablespoons on the fire, or burn them on a shovel.

SKIN

Dry skin can be a problem in summer. Regularly put a teaspoonful of olive oil in the bath water. If your skin is oily, a teaspoonful of epsom salts will have the opposite effect.

SLEEP
Hints for a Good Night's Sleep

■ Stop tossing and turning in bed, waiting for sleep. Use the time for constructive activity. Read, wash clothes, clean out a closet, write letters, watch TV.

■ Make your surroundings conducive to sleep. If the bedroom is too hot or too cold, the bed too lumpy, the pillow too hard, this is distracting. If you are listening to traffic all night instead of sleeping, try earplugs.

■ Maintain a regular schedule of going to bed and getting up. The time of day or night is not important but consistency is.

- Eliminate daytime naps.
- If you are not tired, it will be difficult to sleep. Exercise, even if you only take a walk.
- Do not have coffee or other caffeine drinks before bedtime.
- Although a little bit of alcohol before bedtime may help some people relax, large quantities will cause sleeplessness.
- Sleeping pills can create sleeping problems, so they should be used only occasionally.

SLIMMING

- See *Dieting*.

SMELLS

- See *Odours*.

SNAILS

Snails will not damage seedlings or shrubs if you sprinkle sawdust around the plants. Snails can't crawl over sawdust — it sticks to them.

SOAP

Liquid Soap for Sensitive Clothes

Grate odd ends of toilet soap and dissolve in water over low heat. Use one cup soap to 4 cups water. For laundry-type soap, slice 225 g good laundry soap into an old saucepan and cover with 1200 ml water. Put on stove and heat until dissolved. Do not allow to boil. Cool and store in jars or bottles. This type of soap jelly is good for washing delicate garments, woollens and silks.

Making Sandsoap

One large bar household soap, 1200 ml water, 1200 ml clean white sand, 1200 ml clean white ashes. Cut up soap, put in saucepan with water, stir until soap dissolves. Then stir in sand and ashes. Remove from heat and stir occasionally until mixture sets.

Skin Soap from Leftovers

Save all pieces of scented soap. Cut into shavings. To each cup of shavings, add 2 cups boiling water. It is advisable to stir over heat in saucepan until dissolved. Then add enough fine oatmeal to make a stiff paste and turn into moulds. Next day turn out and shape into required size cakes. When set, which takes a few days, makes a fine skin soap. One cup of soap shavings should make about 12 medium size cakes.

Make Your Own Soap

Place soap pieces in a saucepan with water and bring to boil, stirring occasionally. When cool, puncture a hole in the soap and pour off water. Melt the soap again, without water. Add a tablespoon glycerine, 2 or 3 tablespoons fine oatmeal, and a few drops of perfume. When cold, cut into neat blocks.

Glycerine Soap

Melt scraps of soap by adding a jarful of boiling water to half a jar of scraps. Add juice of a lemon and a teaspoon glycerine. Mix well. Keeps hands beautifully soft.

Soap Sponge

Small scraps of toilet soap can be sewn inside two small squares of foam. Great for lathering children in the bath!

SOUP

■ To sharpen flavour of soup, add half a teaspoon of sugar.
■ Use your mincer for soup vegetables instead of chopping them. Also good for hardened bread when wanted for breadcrumbs.
■ If soup is too salty, add a level teaspoon of brown sugar and boil a thick crust of bread or one large peeled and halved potato with the soup for 15 minutes. Remove crust or potato before serving.
■ Make soups heartier and more nourishing by stirring in 3 tablespoons evaporated milk just before serving.
■ Stir grated cheese into canned or homemade soup just before serving for extra nutrition.
■ Don't throw away vegetable water in which you've cooked celery, carrots or potatoes. Add it to packaged soups instead of water.

SOUR CREAM

Buy cartons or bottles of cream and add 1 dessertspoon of white vinegar. Shake well and use in usual way.

SPECTACLES

Spectacles will be really clean if you polish them with eau-de-cologne.

SPINACH

Make spinach tastier by adding a rasher of chopped bacon while cooking. Add a little butter and pepper before serving.

STAINLESS STEEL

■ Heat marks on stainless steel cooking utensils can be removed by rubbing with fine steel wool and lemon juice.
■ For a good shine on a stainless steel sink, dry and then rub with plain flour, cornflour or bicarbonate of soda using a dry cloth.

STAINS AND MARKS

■ See individual entries like *Clothing*, *Carpet*, etc.

STARCH
Homemade Spray Starch

Mix 1 heaped dessertspoon cornflour in 200 ml cold water, making sure there are no lumps. Stir into 300 ml boiling water and keep stirring until water boils again and mixture thickens. Then pour the mix into 500 ml cold water, using more or less for desired thickness. You now have a litre of spray starch which is as good as the expensive type you buy. A few drops of perfume can be added.

More Effective Starch

When making starch, add one tablespoon kerosene and you'll find the iron runs more smoothly over the garment.

More Homemade Starch

If you run out of starch, make a solution of two tablespoons cornflour to half a cup cold water. Mix to a thin paste, add to 300 ml boiling water. This mixture makes an effective starch.

STEAKS
Two Ways to Tenderise Tough Steak

■ Pour 3 tablespoons salad oil and 1 tablespoon of vinegar into a soup plate, put steak in this for half an hour. Then turn steak over and leave another half hour. Cook as usual for a tenderness like that of choice fillet.
■ Make steak tender by rubbing with lemon juice, Worcestershire sauce or French dressing about one hour before cooking.

Mustard Steak

Before cooking steaks indoors or out, rub first with dry mustard and allow to stand half an hour before cooking.

STEAMED PUDDINGS
Hints for Better Steamed Pud

Grease basin and paper. Accurately weigh or measure all ingredients. Cream butter and sugar thoroughly to ensure fine texture. Add eggs gradually to prevent curdling. Fold in the sifted flour carefully to prevent curdling. Maintain a good volume of steam. Note: in cold weather the creaming process may be hastened by standing the basin in warm water.

STEEL WOOL

To keep steel wool fresh, keep in a jar of water with any old pieces of laundry soap like Sunlight or soap flakes or detergent. Always make sure steel wool is pushed down into soap and completely covered. Change water when necessary.

STEW
Tender Stews

One tablespoon vinegar added to a stew will make the meat more tender.

Thickening a Stew

Add 1 tablespoon oatmeal during cooking for a rich, thickened stew.
■ See recipes under *Cooking*.

STEWED FRUIT

■ Prevent **fruit breaking** or splitting when stewing. Boil the sugar and water together first, then add the fruit to the boiling mixture.
■ **Save sugar** by adding a pinch of bicarbonate of soda added when stewing fruit.
■ For a **thick syrup** when stewing fruit, do not add the usual amount of sugar, but add instead a spoonful of golden syrup when the fruit is nearly done.

Fancy some pink stewed apples?

Add 2 tablespoons of red jelly crystals instead of the sugar. This makes a tasty thick syrup and the apples turn an attractive pink.

STOVES
Stove Polish 1

Mix equal quantities of boiled linseed oil, kerosene and vinegar. Rub stove with a little each day when the stove is cool as this mixture is highly inflammable.

Stove Polish 2

Mix together in a tin 4 cakes black lead, 2 cups turps, 1 dessertspoon washing soda, 1 tablespoon cloudy ammonia, 55 g finely crushed bluestone, 2 tablespoons floor polish. Stir well. Keep in a tightly lidded tin or the turps will evaporate. Apply when stove is cold but do not polish off until stove has warmed up. Can be applied at night and will shine in the morning. Improves the look of black stoves. The bluestone does the trick. Note: bluestone is available at chemists. Take extra care with this as it is a poison.

SUEDE

■ Give suede shoes or handbags a new lease of life by rubbing over with the finest grade sandpaper.
■ Steel wool (the soft-filament variety) is excellent for removing dirt, dust and grease from suede shoes and bags. Also restores the texture to suede.

SUGAR

Soften hardened brown sugar by placing it in a warm oven for a few minutes.

SUNBURN
Two Tips for Relief

■ For mild sunburn, a paste of baking soda and water gives relief.
■ Mix 2 tablespoons each honey, glycerine, lemon juice and 1 tablespoon pure alcohol or toilet water. Put all into a jar and shake until well mixed.

TAPESTRY
Spruce Up Your Tapestry Lounge

■ Use a dry cleaner like Dry Magic which will absorb stains or soiling without causing colours to run. Just rub in with fingers, let dry, then vacuum or brush with light brush. Repeat if necessary.

A 'Bran' New Tapestry

Tapestry stools and chair seats can be cleaned by rubbing vigorously with warm bran.

How to Straighten the Canvas

■ After completing the tapestry, take an old picture frame or piece of wood 25 mm bigger than the canvas. Put 18 mm brads or small head tacks all around about 25 mm apart, then carefully stretch canvas over. Then moisten whole tapestry with water in which 1 tablespoon of alum has been dissolved. This treatment stops moths and silverfish eating the picture or cushion.

■ Another canvas stretcher. Make a thin starch using packet starch and dampen back of tapestry lightly. Stretch over wooden frame and thumb tack edges. Repeat if necessary. Only remove from frame when completely dry.

TARTS
Tasty Caramel

Make a delicious caramel for tarts by putting an unopened can of sweetened condensed milk with a little water in pressure cooker, cook for ½ an hour.

Stop that Shrinking Custard

There are several reasons why custard tarts shrink. The pie plate could be too large. It is also essential that the pastry is not pricked, but glazed with egg white, and that the custard mixture is spooned gently into the pastry case. Warm the milk. It is important not to over-cook a custard tart.

Custard will firm as it cools. When making the custard, I always add two tablespoons full-cream powdered milk to ingredients. The filling cuts beautifully and does not shrink.

The Best Jam Tarts

When using jam to fill tarts, heat almost to boiling point. Pastry will be crisp and never sodden as it often is when cold jam is used.

Never a Sticky Moment

Prevent jam in a tart becoming sticky and dry after baking. Sprinkle the jam liberally with water just before baking.

■ See recipes under *Cooking*.

TEA
A Refreshing Cuppa

Make tea that will really refresh you. Add 3 cloves to the pot with the leaves.

Trick up Your Tea

Improve taste and aroma of tea by putting a little dried orange and lemon rind in the tea packet or jar.

Herbal Teas

■ **Camomile tea**. Measure one cup of water into an enamel saucepan and bring to the boil. Sprinkle one teaspoon of dried camomile heads into the water, put on the lid and boil for ½ a minute. Remove from stove and leave lid on for a little longer so that the valuable essence remains.

■ **Lemon grass tea**. Take a cupful of roughly chopped green tops, immerse in 4 cups boiling water for 4 minutes. Flavour with honey if desired. Dried lemon grass tea is prepared the same way as ordinary tea.

■ **Parsley tea**. Steep 1 teaspoon of parsley leaves and stalks in 1 cup boiling water for 30 minutes.

■ **Decoctin medicinal tea**. Steep 1 level teaspoon parsley seeds in ½ cup boiling water. Take ½ to 1 cup per day. Parsley is extremely rich in vitamins A and C.

TEAK
Goodbye Teak Stains

To remove stains from a teak table, mix table salt and olive oil and rub on. Leave a while. This also makes a good polish though not for lightly polished furniture.

More Stain Removers

Mix olive oil with white vinegar, leave a while then polish with soft cloth. Or rub with a cloth dipped in camphorated oil, or equal parts of linseed oil and turpentine. Use a few drops at a time, keep rubbing, then polish well. Always wondered if cigarette ash had any virtues? Cut a potato in half, coat with cigarette ash, rub over stained teak. Wipe with soft tissue paper

and rub with teak oil or the polish you like best. Remove water stains by rubbing with a block of camphor. This may take some time. Afterwards, rub with a good teak oil.

TEA TOWELS

■ Soak new tea towels in cold water with some Epsom salts. This removes the dressing and makes towels soft and absorbent.

■ When washing tea towels, add a little borax to the water. This disinfectant makes towels a good colour and removes dirt and grease.

TEETH

To remove stains from teeth — not false ones — dip a damp toothbrush in bicarbonate of soda and brush teeth fairly vigorously. Then rinse mouth thoroughly, repeating if necessary. This removes all stains from teeth and makes them sparkling white.

TEETHING RUSKS
Honey Rusks

57 g butter or margarine
57 g sugar
1 tablespoon honey
1 level teaspoon grated lemon rind
113 g flour
¼ level teaspoon baking powder
pinch salt
Cream sugar and shortening, add lemon rind and honey. Fold in sifted dry ingredients, making a dry dough. Roll to a 6 mm thickness on a floured board, cut into finger lengths and place on greased tray. Bake 12 to 15 minutes in moderate oven. Allow to cool on tray and store in airtight tin.

Cheese Rusks

225 g self-raising flour
1 cup grated cheese
110 g butter
1 egg
a little milk

Rub butter into flour, add cheese, mix with egg and milk, to form a dough with the consistency of scone dough. Mark into shapes, cook in fairly hot oven. When half cooked, take slide out of oven and split rusks with fingers. Cook again until nice and brown. Store in airtight tin.

TILES

To clean verandah tiles, mix 300 ml vinegar with 300 ml kerosene. Shake well. Apply with a soft cloth. Also good for marble, lino, furniture, paintwork.

TOFFEE
Hints for Tip Top Toffee

Make sure the sugar is fully dissolved in the liquid before the mixture boils. Wash down the inside of the pan with a pastry brush dipped in cold water or a cloth wrapped around a fork to release any sugar crystals stuck to the pan. Don't stir after the mixture comes to the boil, unless recipe says to stir while cooking. Never make toffee on a damp day, as it will be very sticky. Store wrapped in an airtight container in a cool place, not in the refrigerator.

TOMATOES
Don't Like Acid Tomatoes?

The skins of tomatoes contain the acid, so drop the whole tomatoes into a basin of hot water for a few minutes, then the skin will slip off.

For Shapely Baked Tomatoes

Use small patty pans to bake tomatoes and they will keep their shape.

Tomato Juice

fresh tomatoes, chopped
1 teaspoon worcestershire sauce
1 tablespoon lemon juice
½ teaspoon salt
3 sprigs of parsley (optional)
Blend all the ingredients on high speed for 30 seconds. Keep in a well sealed screwtop jar but not for too long. Pour into glasses when required. Garnish with lemon slices. Serves 4.

Poached Tomatoes

For a delicious change to poached eggs, drop tomato slices in the bottom of the egg poachers. Sprinkle tomato with pepper and salt and allow to heat through before adding eggs.

TOOTHBRUSHES
Recycle that Toothbrush

Don't throw away old toothbrushes. They're great for removing grated lemon, orange and nutmeg from the tiny teeth of your grater. And they're perfect for polishing silver, reaching into grooves where fingers can't. Clean your jewellery with a toothbrush or use it to clean the dust-catching crevices of lamps and elaborately carved furniture. A soft toothbrush can be dipped in detergent and used to clean a badly soiled lampshade.

TOWELS
For Fluffy, Absorbent Towels

Soak towels overnight in warm water with ½ cup of fabric softener in the washing machine. Next morning, run towels through the whole cycle in the same water. Then in plain cold water, wash them for another whole cycle. Dry in a cool place, not in direct sun, or in a tumble dryer on a cool to warm setting. This makes pile much fluffier and the towels more absorbent. After this treatment, towels can be washed in the normal way but should always be rinsed well to ensure fluffiness.

Security Beach Towels

Put a pocket in your beach towel. Turn the corner over and stitch along one side. Insert a zipper in the other side. This is very handy for keys and money.

TOYS
Cleaning Stuffed Toys

A quick, easy and very effective method is to spray with Freedom carpet cleaner. Leave to dry, then brush well. For velvety plush toys, dip cloth in powdered magnesia and rub toys gently. Note: always make sure that all traces of any powder, soap, and so forth used in cleaning are removed, as most soft toys seem to end up in baby's mouth.

TREACLE
Non-Stick Treacle

■ When measuring treacle for a recipe, dip spoon in flour first and the treacle will not stick to it.
■ Dip the spoon in hot water each time you measure treacle. The syrup will drop cleanly from the spoon.

UMBRELLAS

■ Clean by rubbing off any dirt with methylated spirits, then follow with a solution of cold tea and ammonia. To renovate an umbrella, dissolve two tablespoons of sugar in ½ a cup of hot tea and allow to cool. Sponge open umbrella with this solution. The sugar stiffens the fabric and the tea revives the colour.
■ Reproof old umbrellas by painting inside with a little boiled linseed oil. Hang out in sun for 2 days, take in at night.

V

Homemade Vapour Rub with Menthol

1 large jar white petroleum jelly
1 cake natural camphor
1 teaspoon menthol crystals
1½ teaspoons eucalyptus
Melt jelly in small pan, add grated camphor and other ingredients. Store in small screw-topped jars.

Homemade Vapour Rub with Oil

2 tablespoons methylated spirits
4 tablespoons olive oil
4 cakes natural camphor
Melt on slow heat until the mixture boils and thickens, then bottle.

VACUUM FLASKS
Foiling Odours

The cork of a vacuum flask will not affect the taste of its contents if you cover it with foil before sealing.

Goodbye Mustiness

Get rid of that musty smell in vacuum flasks. Add 3 teaspoons bicarbonate of soda to 1 litre warm water and pour into flask. Replace cork and leave about a day. Rinse thoroughly.

VASES
Cleaning Inside Vases

Insides of bottles and vases are easily cleaned with small balls of steel wool and soap suds. A few brisk shakes and they're sparkling.

It Leaks? Fix It Easily

Vases which seep can be painted over inside with clear varnish which makes them waterproof.

VAPOUR RUB
Rubs Require Natural Camphor

Important. Please note you must use the right camphor. There are 2 types: synthetic and natural. Use the natural one, not the synthetic.

Homemade rub

Place 115 g white petroleum jelly on a soup plate and grate into it 2 cakes of natural camphor. Add 3 teaspoonfuls of double distilled eucalyptus. Mix thoroughly and place mixture in jars. Stand jar in hot water on the stove to allow mixture to settle. Keep airtight.

VEGETABLES
Cooking Vegies for One or Two

■ Wrap a small parcel of vegetables in foil and boil them together in one saucepan. Saves fuel, washing up and space on stove, but maintains each flavour.

■ Freshen stale vegetables by soaking them in cold water with one teaspoon of cream of tartar.

■ See recipes under *Cooking*.

VELVET
Cleaning a Velvet Lounge

■ Spray with Freedom carpet cleaner, leave to dry, then vacuum off. A second treatment may be necessary. Cover any wooden areas before treatment.

■ Use a mixture of Shellite and cornflour blended to a cream consistency. Apply with rough cloth like towelling. Rub well into soiled areas. Dry off with clean piece of towelling if too wet. Note. No smoking while using Shellite as it is inflammable.

■ Dip a cloth in powdered magnesia and rub gently.

■ Sponge with equal parts of methylated spirit and water. Test first on piece of velvet on underside of lounge.

■ Sometimes wiping over with a napped or towelling cloth wrung out in warm detergent suds works. Go over surface with a second damp cloth to remove traces of the suds.

VINYL
Goodbye Biro Stains

To remove ballpoint ink from a Nylex vinyl lounge chair, mix equal parts of fresh calcium chloride and fullers earth, both available at your chemist. (Please note, use only calcium chloride as chloride of lime is too drastic and can damage the vinyl.) Now add a few drops of methylated spirits and mix with a knife into a fairly thick paste. Add more methylated spirits as necessary. Apply paste with a knife along the ink stains. Wait for it to dry, then remove with a damp cloth. Finally, wash the affected area over with a wet cloth and dry with a clean cloth. Should stain still remain, repeat cleaning procedure. If removal of the stain leaves the surface dull, wipe over with cottonwool moistened with glycerine. Do not use furniture or floor polishes.

Adios Ads

To remove a printed name from a vinyl travel bag, rub gently with cottonwool ball soaked in acetone (nail polish remover). Turn cottonwool as paint is dissolved and picked up. Always clean surface afterwards with detergent. Caution: acetone is highly inflammable. This method also works on most plastic containers but generally not on glass, where paint is baked on. Or paint over area with brake fluid and let stand. The paint should soften within 30 minutes. Remove with tissue. Repeat until all paint has gone. Clean down with methylated spirits. Don't get brake fluid on any painted surface. Although it works slowly, it is the best non-caustic paint stripper.

Cheerio Grease

To remove greasy stains, lipstick and shoe polish marks from vinyl chairs, remove as much of stain as possible with a dry rag. Take care not to spread the staining substance. Now gently wipe the affected surface with a cotton cloth moistened with methylated spirits or mineral turps. Wash over with warm soapy water.

WALLPAPER
Removing marks and stains

■ Most spots on wallpaper can be removed by rubbing gently with a piece of art gum or stale bread.
■ Clean your wallpaper by rubbing with a ball of plain flour mixed with cleaning fluid. Rub marks gently.
■ To remove blood stains from wallpaper, mix old-fashioned Silver Star starch to a thick paste and cover stain. Leave to dry and when the stain is absorbed, brush it away.
■ Blood stains also succumb to 1 dessertspoon cornflour mixed to a paste with cold water. Spread over stain, leave to dry and brush off.
■ Carbon tetrachloride will remove most grease and blood stains from wallpaper. Mix carbon tetrachloride with magnesia into a paste and spread on wallpaper quickly and liberally with a knife. Leave to

dry. When absolutely dry after several hours, rub powder off with a soft cloth. Repeat if necessary.
■ Remove grease and crayon marks from wallpaper by covering them with a white tissue and pressing with a warm iron. Replace tissues as they absorb stain.

Throw-away Wallpaper Do-dads

Wallpaper oddments cut to shape with pinking shears are a wonderful way to jazz-up trays and dinner tables. Cut lots to fit into all your trays and for cork mats on the dining table. Place them at the bottom of a drawer for a day or two to flatten out. They save hours of washing and ironing since you can just throw them away when stained or soiled.

WALLS
Mildewed Walls? Try These Solutions

■ Wash with strong peroxide (undiluted) about 2 or 3 times. Then paint with an all-purpose sealer.
■ Wash walls with Midco paint cleaner, one part to four of water. When dry, wipe with undiluted methylated spirits. This kills the spores and prevents marks showing through new paint. Ample ventilation is needed to keep mildew from walls. When painting, use one of the brands which contain anti-mould solution.
■ Selley's Painters Sugar Soap, available from hardware stores, is also very good.
■ Use a damp cloth and detergent, then go over with a cloth soaked in neat bleach. Wash down with clean water and mildew will not return.
■ Mix 1 cup each ammonia, disinfectant and detergent and half bucket hot water. Cleans without smears and does not need rinsing off. In the tropics where mildew is a big problem, this solution really removes it.

117

Removing Black Texta Marks

Apply liquid bleach, repeat several times, leave overnight and then wash off. Sometimes Gossamer hair spray is effective.

WALNUTS
Drying Fresh Walnuts

Gather walnuts from the ground soon after they fall. Hull them before the dark bitter fluid of the hulls penetrates the nut meats. Then drop them in water. Rotten and diseased nuts float to the top and should be discarded. To dry the nuts, spread them out rather thinly on a dry, clean surface and allow to dry gradually by exposure to a gentle, but steady movement of air. A cool, darkened and well-ventilated attic or porch is ideal. The nuts need several weeks to dry properly. They are dry enough to be stored when the kernels shake freely in their shells. After drying, nuts still in their shells may be stored for up to a year. Nut meats can be frozen for up to 2 years, as long as they are stored in an airtight container or sealed plastic bag.

Marshmallow Walnuts

Dip walnut halves in marshmallows which have been melted over hot water. Roll them in coconut and chill on waxed paper.

WARTS
A Cure

Warts can often be cured by applying a mixture of equal parts of kerosene, lemon juice and castor oil three times a day for a week.

WASHING CLOTHES
Handy Hints for Fresh Clothes

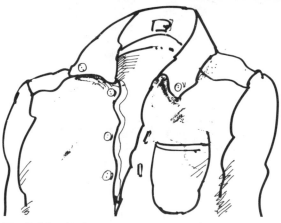

■ Add a little ammonia to soaking water for whites. Will loosen dirt and restore whiteness. Add more to wash water for whiter clothes, to soften and remove grease. Ammonia does not have the harsh effects of bleach.

■ For added sheen on shirt collars, add a small quantity of dissolved epsom salts to the hot water starch.

■ For a grease-resistant finish when washing linen dresses, dissolve one dessertspoon gelatine in hot water and add to rinsing water.

■ Before washing gay florals for the first time, dissolve a packet of epsom salts in cold water and rinse them in this. Then wash in the usual way. The colours will not run.

WASHING LIQUID
Homemade Woolly Washer

225 g Lux flakes
285 ml methylated spirit
2 dessertspoons good eucalyptus
Mix all together in a jar and keep. Flakes do not dissolve. To wash clothes, put 4½ litres warm water in a bowl. Add heaped dessertspoon of flakes and 2 dessertspoons liquid. Leave a few minutes and swish about to dissolve flakes. Put in woollen garments, soak about 5 minutes, longer if very soiled, then press and knead until quite clean. Squeeze out thoroughly and hang to dry. Do not rinse. If water is really dirty, add 2¼ litres clean warm water to the suds already in bowl and wash again in this. Then squeeze and hang to dry.
■ See also *Clothing*.

WATER
Water Softeners

■ Add borax to all washing water, including bath water. There are no problems with the scum of lime when soap is used. Borax can be bought at any chemist.
■ Dissolve 25 g washing soda in just over 500 ml boiling water. Bottle this and use by the tablespoonful as an additive to hard water until the correct degree of softness is obtained. Start with 1 tablespoon per 4½ litres, then add detergent or soapflakes. If water is still too hard, add another tablespoon of the soda solution.

WEEDS

Kerosene sprinkled on paths saves hours of tedious weeding.

WEEVILS
Farewell to these Little Nasties

To keep weevils from flour and stored grains, put a bay leaf in the packet. No more weevils.

WHITEWASH
Old-Fashioned Whitewash No. 1

550 g dry powdered lime, 2.4 litres milk, 2.1 kg whiting. Put lime in an earthenware vessel and pour in enough milk to make a cream, add remainder of milk, pass whiting through a fine sieve into the mixture and stir well. If colour is desired, mix it first with a little milk and then add. The sun does not affect the paint and it will not crack.

Old-Fashioned Whitewash No. 2

5 litres separated milk, 2 kg whiting, 1 cup salt and 1 knob blue. Blend whiting, salt and crushed blue with enough milk to make a paste. Add remainder of milk slowly, stirring well. Strain liquid through hessian or chaff bag and it is ready for use. The same result can be achieved by adding 454 kg skim milk powder to the 4½ litres of water to represent separated milk. Whitewash is permanent, does not flake off and is rain and weatherproof when used outdoors.

WINDOW BOXES

Before adding soil to window boxes, line their bases with several layers of newspaper. The paper stops the soil from drying out too quickly after each watering.

WINDOWS
Cheap, Easy Window Cleaners

■ Use wet newspapers to clean windows most efficiently.
■ Pour left-over tea into a bottle. Add a few drops of glycerine, shake, and use the mixture to clean windows.
■ Kerosene mixed in equal parts with methylated spirits and water makes an excellent window cleaner fluid. Keep in a screw-top jar. Wipe over windows with liquid on clean cloth. Allow to dry, then polish with newspaper or clean cloth.
■ For a clean sparkle, add a little ammonia to water when washing windows.

Prevent Steamed Windows

■ Rub with a cloth soaked in equal quantities glycerine and methylated spirits. Or rub window with dry soap and polish briskly with a dry clean cloth until soap stains are removed.

Making Windows Opaque

To blot out unwelcome sights, wipe each glass window with a cloth dampened in methylated spirits to remove all traces of grime and dirt. Then apply plastic wall paint to the inside of the glass, using a small roller. The wet paint can be stippled by dabbing it with any kind of paint brush. You can make another type of frosting but it is less durable. Dissolve 250 g epsom salts in 1 cup boiling water and paint on to the glass while mixture is still hot. Crystals will form as the solution cools. Epsom salts can also be added to white paint to give a frosty look. After application, stipple the surface to make brush marks less obvious.

Opening Paint Jammed Windows

■ If your windows are a sash type — the ones that slide up and down on rope and pulleys — get a pinch bar or jemmy and insert between window and jamb, tapping with a hammer to drive the jemmy in about 12 mm.
 By applying pressure, the sash will move across the window space breaking the paint line. Do this on both sides, then slide the sash up and down about 20 times to wear away the paint. If the window still sticks, buy products like Dry Lube, surf board wax or Rub Candle, and apply where sash rides in the channel.
■ For hopper type windows, you need a block of wood and a hammer. Undo the latches and tap all along the stile where the latch holds the window closed. When you finally get windows open, run a file along the lumps of paint to remove.

WINDSCREENS
Make Windscreens Shine

Mix baking powder to a thin paste with water. Rub on the screen, rinse off, dry, then polish with a soft cloth.

Remove Wiper Scratches

Brasso polishes and removes light scratches. Toothpaste is also often effective. Apply and polish off with dry cloth. Apply a second time, leave to dry, then polish off with crushed pieces of newspaper.

WOODEN BLOCKS
Restore Kiddies' Blocks Without Paint

Peg a piece of medium glasspaper to a flat piece of board with six drawing pins, one in each corner, and one each on the long sides to stop the paper moving. Using an up and down motion across the paper, clean off all the paint. Colour the blocks with cake icing dye from the confectionery counter of some large stores. This is an edible dye causing no ill effects when blocks are sucked by toddlers. Stain by pouring dye on a damp cloth and rubbing well into the wood. Place in the sun to dry. Surplus can be wiped off with a wet cloth.

WOOL

To **revive old balls of wool** which have become grubby and musty smelling, wind wool into skeins using the back of a chair. Tie skeins twice with contrasting coloured wool, leaving enough to attach the skeins to the clothes line. Tying them keeps from tangling while being washed. Wash in fairly hot water with this mixture: 226 g Lux flakes, 283 ml methylated spirits and 2 dessertspoons eucalyptus. Shake together in jar. Soap powder can be used instead but the mixture is best. Rinse in cold water. Squeeze out dry in a towel and hang on line on a good drying day. Leave until dry, rewind into balls. This takes out all crinkles and musty smells. Note: do not spin dry.

WOOLLEN GARMENTS
Soft, Silky Woollens

Dissolve 60 g borax in a 1 litre jug of hot water, pour this into 4 litres tepid water, add 1 teaspoon vinegar. Soak woollens in this for 5 minutes. Washes and softens in one go.

Want a Smaller Lambswool Pullover?

Put garment on person and pin seams in as required. Use blackberry pins if possible. Take in evenly through sides and, if necessary, through armhole seams and down sleeve seams. Stitch twice, stretching as you sew. Then stitch again 3 cm from finished seam and cut off excess near this last row of stitching. Press lightly with steam iron to get rid of stretching and neaten edge on basque.

Restretch Shrunken Woollens

Soak garments in water with 85 g Epsom salts. Dissolve the salts in boiling water and allow to cool. Leave garments soaking for ½ an hour, remove, squeeze out excess water and pull back into right shape. When almost dry, press under a dry cloth.

Prevent Stretched Cuffs

To prevent stretching, simply knit in elastic thread as you knit the cuffs, basques, sock tops and so forth. Do not use the carded type but the elastic thread sold by the metre. This is soft and fine and obtainable at knitting or haberdashery counters in a variety of shades. The elastic can be replaced with a bodkin type needle if washing and wear make it loose.

No More Fluff

Prevent angora and lambswool jumpers shedding fluff. Simply put in a plastic bag in the coldest section of the fridge overnight before wearing. This will set the fluff. Knitters who find fluff gets up their noses while knitting angora or lambswool should put balls of yarn in a plastic bag in the fridge.

Remedy for Matted Wool

To renovate a woollen cardigan that is thick and unwearable from bad washing, try mixing 1 tablespoon each eucalyptus, Lux flakes and methylated spirit with enough lukewarm water to rinse the cardigan thoroughly. Wring lightly but do not use further rinsing water. Hang out in shade.

Goodbye Shiny Trousers

Ammonia will remove shine from woollen and worsted garments and seats of well-worn trousers. Just sponge shiny areas with an ammonia and water solution, then press with a damp cloth and warm iron.

Yellowed Wool?

For woollen garments which have yellowed with age, rub over with a brush dipped in ammonia. This restores original freshness.

Whiten Woollies

To restore a white hand knitted woollen vest, buy a tin of Dylon Super White from the chemist and follow directions on label. This will restore the garment to white. Then wash using either powdered borax or Fiesta in the washing water. Turn garment inside out when putting out to dry and always dry in the shade. This way, you'll have no more worries about keeping the garment white.

A Different Moth Repellant

Instead of putting camphor or mothballs among woollens, sprinkle oil of cinnamon on little pieces of cotton wool and place among the clothes.

Recycle Old Socks

Old woollen socks make excellent polishing cloths. Just slip one on each hand.

WROUGHT IRON

Prevent rust forming on wrought iron furniture by applying a coat of liquid wax when new, and again from time to time.

YEAST
Bakers Yeast

1 small handful hops
1200 ml cold water
6 level tablespoons each flour and sugar
   Boil hops and water together for 20 minutes or until hops fall to the bottom. Strain and allow to cool. Blend flour and sugar, using a little of the hop liquor. Stir all well together. Bottle and cork and tie well down. Stand in a warm place. Ready to use in 24 hours.

Brewers Yeast

28 g hops
2 medium sized potatoes
1.7 litres water
2 tablespoons sugar
1 cup plain flour

Boil hops, sliced potatoes and water for 20 minutes, strain and add sugar. Allow to get quite cold. Mix flour with a little of the liquid, add to rest of the yeast and bottle. Cork well, using a seasoned bottle. The first difficulty in making yeast is to get a well seasoned bottle. It's a good plan to brew yeast in small quantities several times in the same bottle, leaving a little of the old brew in each time. In summer the yeast requires 8 to 10 hours to ripen; in winter from 20 to 24 hours.

Simple Yeast

3 tablespoons plain flour
2 tablespoons sugar
   Mix to a paste with half cup lukewarm water. Seal mixture in an airtight jar. Allow to stand in warm place until fermented, which takes about 48 hours. Yeast is now ready for use. To keep yeast working, feed every other night with 2 tablespoons flour, 1 tablespoon sugar and ¾ cup lukewarm water mixed to a paste.

ZIPPERS

Lubricate a sticky zipper by rubbing well with candle wax, paraffin, a bar of soap or ordinary pencil lead. Talc also works sometimes.

BBR 92   Printed in HONG KONG